# Books by Corey Ford

## Parody

THREE ROUSING CHEERS
MEANING NO OFFENSE
SALT WATER TAFFY
THE JOHN RIDDELL MURDER CASE
COCONUT OIL
IN THE WORST POSSIBLE TASTE
THE DAY NOTHING HAPPENED

## Humor

THE GAZELLE'S EARS (*anthology*)
THE HORSE OF ANOTHER COLOR
HOW TO GUESS YOUR AGE
THE OFFICE PARTY
NEVER SAY DIET
HAS ANYBODY SEEN ME LATELY? (*anthology*)
COREY FORD'S GUIDE TO THINKING
WHAT EVERY BACHELOR KNOWS
AND HOW DO WE FEEL THIS MORNING?

## War Books

FROM THE GROUND UP (*with Alastair MacBain*)
SHORT CUT TO TOKYO
WAR BELOW ZERO
CLOAK AND DAGGER (*with Alastair MacBain*)
THE LAST TIME I SAW THEM (*anthology*)

## Outdoors

A MAN OF HIS OWN (*wtih Alastair MacBain*)
EVERY DOG SHOULD HAVE A MAN
YOU CAN ALWAYS TELL A FISHERMAN
MINUTES OF THE LOWER FORTY
UNCLE PERK'S JUG

## History and Biography

A PECULIAR SERVICE
WHERE THE SEA BREAKS ITS BACK
THE TIME OF LAUGHTER

# THE
# TIME
# OF
# LAUGHTER

# THE TIME OF LAUGHTER

## by Corey Ford

*with a Foreword by* FRANK SULLIVAN

*Little, Brown and Company* · Boston · Toronto

LIBRARY OF CONGRESS CATALOG CARD NO. 67-21098

FIRST EDITION

We are grateful for permission to use the following copyrighted material
and illustrations:

Selections from Robert Benchley's "Horse Sense Editorial," published in
the old *Life;* from "The Treasurer's Report," published in *The Treasurer's
Report and Other Aspects of Community Singing* by Robert Benchley, Copyright 1930 by Robert Benchley; and from other writings of Robert Benchley.
Reprinted by permission of Mrs. Robert Benchley and of Nathaniel Benchley.

Caricature of Harold Ross by Al Hirschfeld, published in *The Vicious
Circle* by Margaret Harriman, 1951. Reprinted by permission of Al Hirschfeld.

Selections from "Odd's Bodkins" by Ring Lardner, published in *The New
Yorker.* Copyright © 1933, 1961 by The New Yorker Magazine, Inc. Reprinted by permission of the author and of The New Yorker.

Shortened version of "I Gaspiri" from *First and Last* by Ring Lardner.
Copyright 1934 by Ellis A. Lardner; renewal copyright © 1962 Ring Lardner, Jr. Reprinted with the permission of Charles Scribner's Sons.

Selections from the old *Life* magazine: a letter from Edward Stratemeyer,
a cartoon by T. S. Sullivant, a posed photograph from the old *Life*'s "News-
Stand" parody issue, and a posed photograph from the old *Life*'s "Daily
Life" parody issue. Reprinted by permission of the copyright holder, Henry
Trowbridge Rockwell.

*Published simultaneously in Canada
by Little, Brown & Company (Canada) Limited*

PRINTED IN THE UNITED STATES OF AMERICA

*For*
*Dorothy Olding*

# Foreword

THE TIME OF LAUGHTER. It is a proper title for Corey Ford's account of New York and Hollywood in the Twenties and early Thirties, that lively era before the storm clouds gathered. Ford himself was a cause of a good deal of the laughter of that time. I can think of no American humorist who excelled him in the subtle art of parody. The parodies of the then current best sellers he wrote for *Vanity Fair* under the name of John Riddell are still fresh in the memory of readers they delighted. (They did not usually amuse the authors of the books he impaled.) I wish he were in a mood to take on some of the stark novels of today, the output of the solemn, humorless emancipators of the four-letter words, so like little boys chalking dirty words on sidewalks.

Ford has done an entertaining job of recalling the years he has chosen to chronicle; the fun-makers and humorists of those days, and the world they moved in. I cannot think of an ornament of the period he has not placed in the proper niche and to whom he has not given proper appreciation. It was a pleasant time on the whole, full of agreeable souls who had a lot of fun along with their share of cares, and were not unduly

*Carl Howard*

Frank Sullivan, Ford's "Ugly Roomer."

given to self-pity. I doubt if Shakespeare and Ben Jonson at the Mermaid Tavern, or Samuel Johnson and Sir Joshua Reynolds at the Mitre, had any more fun or any more good fellowship than Mr. Benchley, Harold Ross, Heywood Broun, Marc Connelly, and their friends had at the Algonquin, Bleeck's, Moriarty's, and "21."

Things were not all gas and gaiters. Some of us did stretches on analysts' couches. We didn't swallow tranquilizers at the rate popular today for the good reason that there weren't any tranquilizers. I don't know that any of the circle Ford writes about took any drug more potent than a sleeping pill. If they did they did not brag about it, as the fashion is today among the reefer set. Unless of course you count bootleg gin as a drug. Most of us were able to hold our fair share of that, or of Scotch, and the bootleggers could not have poisoned their wares too drastically, because we survived. The relic who pens these lines is still around, as of this writing, turning contentedly to stone at what some wag has termed a Ripe Old Age.

We lived in a fool's paradise, or on the edge of a volcano; take your choice. We thought, those of us who gave the matter any thought, that there would be no more world wars. Hadn't many of us just fought in a war to end war? Our spirits would have tobogganed if we had had to reckon with the Sword of Damocles that has hung over the world since Hiroshima. In these days an old man tries to remember this when tempted to impatience with the odd behavior of the young generation. God help them, they are having a more anxious time of it, and face a tougher world, than their fathers or their grandfathers did. One can only pray that when they take over they will do a better job on the world than their elders have done.

Corey Ford had scarcely cast his first vote when he attracted national attention with his Rover Boy parodies in *Life* magazine, though he had attracted some local attention on Morningside Heights even earlier when he wrote a piece for the Columbia *Jester* calling Nicholas Murray Butler a jackass. He was a part of the scene he describes in this book; he was a member of the wedding. He knew just about all of the men and women he writes about here. He was to be found with his cronies at The Players or the Coffee House or the Dutch Treat Club or, in Hollywood, at Chasen's and the Garden of Allah. And he was by no means a stranger to the speakeasy life of that day, although he played the speakeasies more temperately than some of his fellow jesters did. I particularly envy him his friendship with the immortal W. C. Fields, whom he celebrates in a hilarious and affectionate chapter.

One morning Ford awoke to find, to his astonishment, that he had reached middle age. Sighing, he decided he might as well cash in on this doleful milestone, so he sat himself at a typewriter and wrote a brief but mighty funny treatise called "How to Guess Your Age." I regret he has not in this book gone into his adventures with "How to Guess Your Age." It was not only widely read, it was widely stolen. It was swiped wholesale throughout the land by hijackers who read it, loved it, and had thousands of copies of it struck off and sent to friends as something they had tossed off in a leisurely moment. Not a word of credit to Ford in all this. It was also stolen by a few professionals who should have known better, the crooks. The experience brought home to Ford the widely held view in this country that writing is not really work and that humor especially is slightly infra dig. When Ford set his lawyer on a few of these plagiarists (he couldn't possibly deal with all of them) they were amazed to find there was anything illegal in stealing a piece of writing. They could not believe that a writer's handiwork is as much a piece of property as a filling station. "You call writing *work!*" Why, they could dash off something as good as "The Snows of Kilimanjaro" any afternoon they chose to spare from the golf course. Ford would rate high in Dun and Bradstreet today if he had been able to collect royalties from all these stolen reprints of "How to Guess Your Age." He still winces at the memory of that wholesale larceny.

He has touched on the subject in this book but I ask indulgence to discourse further on the apartment he and I shared during the first half of the Thirties, and to mention some minor points he forgot. The apartment was on East 51st Street, at the head of Beekman Place. Beekman Place was then a charming two-block backwater in mid-Manhattan. We had lovely neighbors. Patricia Collinge, the actress, lived across the street. Guthrie McClintic and Katharine Cornell (Mrs. McClintic) lived a few doors down the Place. So did Margalo Gillmore, Ruth Hammond, and Donald Macdonald. The James Forrestals and the Robert Lovetts lived there, neither Mr. Forrestal nor Mr. Lovett foreseeing that in a few years they would be serving their country so greatly and so honorably. Lillian and Dorothy Gish lived in the apartment house just east of us, and we had only to cross a courtyard to visit Aleck Woollcott, Alice Duer Miller, and the Ralph Pulitzers. It was a friendly neighborhood, as sequestered as if it were a hundred miles from Broadway.

Not that life was monastically calm there, at least not in our apartment. One time a maid in the adjoining apartment house saw Ford working in his study and fell in love with him through the windows, just like a heroine in an O. Henry story. She wrote him love letters, which went unanswered. It was very romantic and his friends told Ford it was, but he wouldn't believe us, and snarled whenever we brought the matter up — which we did pretty constantly. Occasionally some of his brothers from the Deke house at Columbia would come home with Ford after a night on the town and if I wasn't already home and in bed — and I seldom was — they would pie my bed. My, my, it took me right back to my student days at Cornell.

I had the apartment to myself half the time because Ford was away half the time. He was a human dynamo, constantly on the move. I was averse to travel, holding with Dr. Johnson that the man who is tired of London is tired of life, save that New York was my London. Sometimes, in rash moments, I would determine to throw a few things into a bag and travel somewhere, to broaden my horizon. Then I would ask myself, "Is this trip necessary?" and Echo — bless her! — always answered, "No." But Ford was never happier than when flying over the Himalayas, or catching salmon in Alaska, or collecting virgins in Bali. For my part the happiest trip he made during our partnership was one to Bimini. I forget why he felt he had to go to Bimini, but I remember that it was there he met the paragon of all bootleggers, a courtly and agreeable entrepreneur whom we instantly appointed our house apothecary. We entered into a business arrangement with this Samaritan. For a consideration he periodically packed a trunk very carefully with a store of the choicest wines and liquors and expressed it to our apartment. We drank high off the hogshead that winter. We hadn't tasted such rare potations since ante-Volstead days, and not often even then. About three of the trunks reached us intact, and were shipped back to our man in Bimini for restocking. The next trunk arrived one day when Ford was away and I was in residence. The doorman called my attention to the fact that the trunk seemed curiously light. It was indeed, and with good reason. It was empty. Somewhere along its journey it must have gurgled at the wrong moment. It had been opened and hijacked of its nectars. We returned the empty trunk sorrowfully to our Bimini friend. Not long afterward repeal came and he went out of business with, I hope, a handsome nest egg put by for his old age.

In those years Ford had another domicile in Freedom, New Hampshire, and he went there incessantly to fish or hunt or work, or all three. He had visited Freedom in earlier years and had liked it so well that he determined to build a modest hideout there to which he could flee when New York got him down. Just a shack, you know. Nothing pretentious. Then he consulted an architect and the fun began. Consultations took place almost daily. Improvements and curlicues crept slyly into the plans for the modest shack, and pretty soon the shack got lost in the shuffle. I, the Ugly Roomer, was an innocent and awestruck bystander to all this frenzy, acting as a wailing wall to Ford at times when it looked as if the erstwhile modest shack would bankrupt him. When he and the architect came down to earth Ford found himself the lord of a baronial castle, replete with silver faucets in the bathrooms and other decadent luxuries, all at a cost of about fifty thousand dollars. He had planned to spend three or four thousand dollars.

I bowed out as wailing wall when Ford spent another small fortune to import trees from some distant forest to help landscape his Freedom estate. Importing *trees* to New Hampshire, one of the woodsiest states in the Union! I forbear to mention coals to Newcastle, but it was a wonder the government of New Hampshire didn't send him packing back to York State, where everybody is crazy.

Ford enjoyed his white elephant for a number of years, then tired of it and sold it at a sacrifice, and with some difficulty. He moved to the livelier and more congenial Hanover, to which to date he has not imported any trees, nor, as far as I know, any snow in January.

The syndicated philosophers tell us of the geriatric bloc not to dwell upon the past. Live for today, they urge. Well, a hell of a today to live for is all I can say. I plan to dwell on the past anytime I choose, especially the past Corey Ford recounts here, and I thank him for reviving a charming era so vividly, and bringing to life so many lively and dear people, with whom I have laughed and drunk and argued and in general made the welkin ring.

The welkins you hear ringing today sound flat to me.

FRANK SULLIVAN

# Contents

# List of Illustrations

# THE
# TIME
# OF
# LAUGHTER

# 1

## *A Time for Laughter*

NEW YORK in the Roaring Twenties — and they were my
twenties, too — was a magic town to be young in. Any
morning I could open the *World* and brighten my day with
F.P.A.'s "Conning Tower" or Heywood Broun's "It Seems to
Me" or Frank Sullivan's "Out of a Clear Sky." I would haunt
the corner newsstand until the *Sun* arrived, in order to follow
the adventures of Archy and Mehitabel in Don Marquis's
"Sun Dial." Alexander Woollcott was writing theatrical reviews for the *Times*, the "Alibi Ike" stories by Ring Lardner
were running in the *Saturday Evening Post,* and bookstores
offered the latest works of P. G. Wodehouse and George S.
Chappell and Donald Ogden Stewart. Each week *Life* carried
a drama criticism by Robert Benchley (imagine reading a
Benchley piece for the first time) and a movie column by
Robert E. Sherwood and sometimes a new poem by Dorothy
Parker.

Or I could take the subway down to Times Square, and buy a
balcony seat to see W. C. Fields in person as the magnificent
mountebank in *Poppy,* trying to play the kadoula-kadoula while
his ubiquitous midget walked past him with squeaky shoes, or

assuring Madge Kennedy in that inimitable nasal drawl, "You're the fondest girl I am of." A block away, Will Rogers's lariat was lassooing popular shibboleths at the *Follies*, and Fannie Brice was singing a haunting ballad called "My Man." I could drop in on Ed Wynn Himself in *The Perfect Fool*, or Joe Cook and Dave Chasen in Earl Carroll's *Vanities*, or the Four Marx Brothers in *I'll Say She Is*, or Roland Young in George Kaufman and Marc Connelly's *Beggar on Horseback*. I could visit the neighborhood movie theaters and watch the silent clowns of Hollywood: Charles Chaplin in *The Gold Rush*, Buster Keaton in *The Navigator*, Harold Lloyd in *Safety Last*.

Everywhere around me I could sense the emanations of greatness, the proximity of giants which made a stroll in the city intriguing and full of promise. I would walk slowly along Forty-fourth Street past the Algonquin Hotel, and picture to myself the scintillating wits seated at that very moment around its fabled Round Table. I came to know them all in time; but somehow it was more exciting to imagine myself brushing elbows with them unwittingly in the crowd, to glance at a stranger in a theater lobby and wonder if he might be Woollcott or Benchley or F.P.A. One afternoon on a Fifth Avenue bus a friend pointed out Dorothy Parker (it turned out later that he was mistaken) and once, loitering at the corner of Chambers Street and Broadway, I saw Don Marquis climb out of a taxi and hurry into the *Sun* building, perhaps to determine whether the poetic cockroach had left another complaint in his type-writer about the quality of office crumbs.

This, then, is a sentimental journey back to that distant decade, the Golden Age of American Humor. The early Twenties marked the peak of comic writing in this country, a flowering of satire and parody and sheer nonsense that has never been equaled before or since, a galaxy of our greatest funnymen gathered together at one transcendent moment like a configuration of planets which would not occur again in a lifetime. By today's standards, I suppose, their comedy might seem unsophisticated and obvious. Much of it was bigger-than-life, the flying custard pie, the snowball aimed at the top hat; but it was happy, and wholesome, and there was no malice concealed in a joke like a rock in the snowball. Fun had only one purpose, and that was to be funny. Humor was its own excuse.

Memory has a way of oversimplifying the past; and it must be conceded, in honesty, that the decade was loud and rude and crass, largely concerned with making money, making love, making whoopee. The roar of the Twenties was discordant, a raucous cacophony of wailing saxophones and snapping fingers and feet stamping the Black Bottom, staccato of guns in a Chicago gang war, crash of broken bottles in a Prohibition raid, extras crying the Hall-Mills murder, the boom in Florida, the bomb in Wall Street; but at least we could laugh at ourselves, we could make fun. Whatever else may be said of the era — and certainly it was materialistic and self-centered — it was a time for laughter.

# 2

## When I Was One-and-Twenty

I was just finishing my freshman year at Columbia, that spring of 1920, when Scott Fitzgerald's *This Side of Paradise* exploded over every college campus. I read it avidly; we all did. After all, he was writing about our own generation (it was the first time I'd thought of myself as belonging to a "generation") and we were surprised and rather flattered to learn that we had "grown up to find all Gods dead, all wars fought, all faiths in man shaken."

This was heady stuff for a teen-ager, and we set our freshman caps at a rakish angle and leered at our reflections in the mirror. Most of us had come from strait-laced homes, reared in the confining mold of Victorian precepts, and it was exhilarating to conceive of ourselves as dissolute and decadent members of the Jazz Age, to be denounced in editorials as a threat to "the stability of our American civilization." So we were a National Problem. Well, we would do our best to live up to our reputation. When Gertrude Stein called us "the lost generation," we carried the phrase aloft like a banner.

Fitzgerald christened it the Jazz Age, but John Held, Jr., set its style and manners. His angular and scantily clad flapper was accepted by scandalized elders as the prototype of modern youth, the symbol of our moral revolution. Frankly I had never seen anything remotely resembling that fantastic female until Held's derisive pen portrayed her. My guess is that she sprang full-blown from his imagination: flat-chested, long spidery legs ending in stubby feet like hooves, her brief skirt riding high to reveal the rolled top of a stocking and a glimpse of flesh, cloche hat on close-bobbed hair, a precise dot of rouge below each cheekbone and a matching crimson mouth. *Betty Co-Ed has lips of red for Hah-vud.* Out of the same whole cloth he created her moon-faced escort, with outsize coonskin coat, bell-bottom trousers sagging over his shoes, patent-leather hair, polka-dot bow tie, a hip flask in one hand and the wheel of a Stutz Bearcat in the other. *C'llegiate! C'llegiate! Yes, we are collegiate!*

Imaginary or real, Held's sheiks and shebas became a national vogue. Week after week, in *Life* and *Judge* and *College Humor,* they danced the Charleston with ropes of beads swinging and bracelets clanking and legs kicking at right angles, or trudged across the campus in unbuckled galoshes and yellow slickers autographed with nicknames and Greek fraternity letters. He showed them necking in pairs on the rising treads of a staircase beside a deserted ballroom floor (*The Dance-Mad Younger Set,* the ironic caption read). A couple sprawled in amorous embrace on a golf course to the annoyance of an approaching older player (*One Up, Two to Go*). A bewildered flapper searching for a blind date in a crowd of identical fur-clad collegians (*He told her he'd be wearing a raccoon coat*). An angular female puffing smoke defiantly from a ten-inch cigarette holder (*She left home under a cloud*). Sometimes his satire turned savage, as in his portrayal of a chinless Joe College with the caption: *One mother, one father, one tonsil-expert, four general practitioners, three trained nurses, five governesses, fifty-six ordinary teachers, thirty-two*

*professors, and three athletic trainers combined their efforts to
produce this.*

Perhaps no comic artist ever had a more immediate impact on
a generation. Bearing out Oscar Wilde's contention that nature
imitates art, we took his exaggerated cartoon types to heart and
patterned ourselves on them. Each new Held drawing was pored
over like a Paris fashion plate, girls cropped their hair and
rouged their cheeks and shortened their skirts to be in style,
galoshes and raccoon coats were indispensable to every male
undergraduate wardrobe. So sedulously did we ape his caricatures that they lost their satiric point and came to be a docu-
mentary record of our times.

All this collegiate adulation was a source of sour amusement
to John Held, Jr., who had never been to college. He was in fact
the very antithesis of the characters he drew: darkly handsome,
quiet and withdrawn, with a pulled-down scornful smile. He
disliked clamorous cocktail parties, and the acidity of his cartoons was due in large part to a withering contempt for the
boop-boop-a-doop products of the Jazz Age. "Just because I
draw them," he told me once, "doesn't mean I have to like
them." He vastly preferred dogs and horses and, as his success
mounted and the money rolled in, he retired to Connecticut to
lead the life of a country squire, far removed from the roar of
the Twenties. Here he indulged in his hobby of sculpture,
fashioned woodcuts and linoleum blocks, hammered out
wrought-iron fixtures on his home forge, and wrote a total of
eight books in three years; but he could never live down his
earlier reputation, and was known best as the delineator of the
younger set he detested.

I learned this much later, of course. John Held had not yet
sold a magazine cover when I entered Columbia in the fall of
1919. It was a strange mixture, that first postwar class. Fully a
third were A.E.F. veterans who had resumed their schooling

after a couple of years in the muddy trenches of Normandy. Some of them were my own age, but infinitely older in experience, war-hardened and callous. My roommate arrived a month late — he had been doing occupational duty on the Rhine — and his crass army philosophy shocked my innocent ears: "Love 'em where you find 'em, and leave 'em where you love 'em." "Grab it when you can, Jack." "You're a long time dead." The ashtray on his desk was an inverted German helmet punctured with two holes, one small, one larger and jagged. I asked him where he got it. "A Heinie was wearing it," he said casually; and I looked in embarrassment at the college pennant over my own desk, and realized the impossible gulf between us. There had been different moral standards overseas, mademoiselles from Armentières were available and easily had, and he could not readjust to this prim old-fashioned world of restrictions and taboos. Night after night he would come back to our room gloriously drunk, boasting of his newest sexual conquest. "How ya gonna keep 'em down on the farm," he would sing at the top of his lungs while I helped him off with his clothes, "after they've seen Paree? . . ."

He quit school before his freshman term was over; only a handful of veterans stuck it out for four full years, but while they lasted they made a dominant impression on the rest of us. We tried to emulate their hard-boiled hedonism, and scoffed at everything which had formerly seemed important and true. I had written some poetry before coming to college, but now I hid the poems in a bottom drawer, and turned to parody and satire to show off my newly acquired cynicism, to win approval in their eyes. At the start of my sophomore year I was elected editor of the college comic magazine, the Columbia *Jester,* and when I entered the fraternity house for lunch that day they rose and cheered me, the first time I had ever been cheered. I think that was the moment I decided to become a humorist. Overwhelmed by their acclaim, I redoubled my efforts to be the campus rebel, laid about me indiscriminately with the fool's bladder, and in my first issue called President Nicholas Murray Butler a jackass. President Butler showed remarkable forbearance (though he pointed out rather stiffly that he didn't agree with me) and refrained from tossing me out of school. I suppose he had resigned himself to the fact that good manners were out of date, that this was an age of iconoclasm, a time of disenchantment.

Back in the Twenties the college comics were in their heyday, an invaluable proving ground for budding humor writers. As editor of the *Jester,* I followed in the distinguished footsteps of Bennett Cerf and Howard Dietz and H. W. Hanemann. Robert Benchley and Gluyas Williams and Robert Sherwood had graduated from the Harvard *Lampoon,* Cole Porter and Peter Arno from the Yale *Record.* S. J. Perelman edited the Brown *Jug* the year after I graduated, Joseph Bryan III ran the Princeton *Tiger,* and Hugh Troy was on the Cornell *Widow.* Theodor Geisel was turning out weird and wonderful cartoons signed "Dr. Seuss" for the Dartmouth *Jack-o-Lantern,* and James Thurber first drew his doleful dogs for the Ohio State *Sun-Dial.*

The Columbia *Jester* was happily located in New York City, center of the professional world of humor. Taking advantage of our strategic position, we decided to publish a Celebrities Issue of *Jester,* made up of contributions from every famous artist and writer whom we could browbeat for free copy. Frank de Sales Casey, the genial art editor of *Life,* supplied us with addresses and private numbers, and we wrote a series of obsequious letters in which the word "grateful" occurred at least four times, nagged our victims mercilessly over the telephone, even made personal calls at their studios to wheedle a poem or bit of artwork gratis. It was a brash imposition on their good nature; but it never occurred to me, until I became a professional myself, that a craftsman cannot afford to turn out less than his best, that we were asking them to make us a gift of material which they could have sold for profit. They responded with uniform generosity, and we assembled a magazine so full of expensive names that Frank Casey observed ruefully, *"Life* couldn't afford to put out an issue like that."

It was a remarkable issue, as I glance over it now, a complete anthology of the comedy of the Twenties. The cover was by Coles Phillips, then the highest paid advertising artist in the country. Charles Dana Gibson presented us with one of his legendary Gibson Girls, dressed as the Columbia Alma Mater and inscribed "To the *Jester* with every good wish." Don Marquis appropriately led off the magazine with a satiric essay entitled "There Aren't Any Celebrities." George Chappell, as Dr. Walter E. Traprock, wrote a hitherto unpublished chapter from *The Cruise of the Kawa,* decorated by Ralph Barton with a precise caricature of Heywood Broun as Captain Ezra Triplett. The inimitable Gluyas Williams drew a full-page series of cartoons called "Portrait of an Earnest Student Pursuing Knowledge." (I could never have imagined that two years later Gluyas Williams would illustrate my first book.)

Our Table of Contents was a virtual Who's Who of American humor. George S. Kaufman wrote an original satiric verse, illustrated by Charles Baskerville. John Held, Jr., sent us a panel of his flappers, viewed from all angles. Wallace Irwin and Rea Irvin collaborated on a Hashimura Togo letter entitled "Japanese Schoolboy Sends Greetings," which was addressed "To Editor Columbia Gesture" and concluded: "I should be delicious to write you some international sporting news about human races, etc., but am prevented by my ignorance. Hoping you are the same, Yours truly." Donald Ogden Stewart contributed a parody of children's books called "How the Twink

A John Held contribution to the Columbia *Jester* Celebrities Issue.

Family Learned about Sex." Ring Lardner submitted a piece of pure nonsense, in that sublime style which no one else has ever been able to approach. "Bugs Baer's Comeback," it was titled, and it began solemnly:

As a rule humorists are notoriously dull and trite in conversation. An exception to this rule is Bugs Baer, the famous author of "Polly-anna" and the Pansy books. Recently Mr. Baer was engaged in a game of bridge on the verandah of the fashionable Commercial House at Duluth, where he spends his winters. One of the players was a Paraguese who could say only a few words of English. . . .

The pageant of Celebrities went on and on. There was a telegram of rhymed regrets reading: FORGIVE ME, PLEASE, I MEANT TO SEND A CONTRIBUTION SORELY. ASHAMED AND GRIEVED, I AM YOUR FRIEND, YOUR FAITHLESS FRIEND, CHRISTOPHER MORLEY. A curt handwritten refusal from Irvin S. Cobb (our only turndown) which we reproduced along with a devastating portrait by Tony Sarg captioned "Picture of Irvin S. Cobb Being Too Busy to Contribute to *Jester.*" A two-page spread by T. S. Sullivant, whose Neanderthal men and sagging cows were favorites of both *Life* and *Punch*. A cartoon of Columbia's long-suffering President Butler by Al Frueh, with an imaginary interview by Thomas L. Masson. Drawings by George Herriman, creator of the immortal *Krazy Kat,* Percy (*Skippy*) Crosby, and Reginald (*Little Lord Fauntleroy*) Birch. And, as a fitting climax, an "Ode from Horace" by F.P.A., the particular god of every would-be writer:

*The Simple Bard*
Horace: Book 1, Ode 38
*"Persicos odi, puer, apparatus—"*

Three bucks a line? No, not for mine.
I care no tittle for emolum-
Ents and returns—the kind one earns
Writing a colyum.

"What, moving, Mrs. Turtle?"
"Yes, we couldn't stand it another day — our apartment is
simply full of musk rats . . ."

Cartoon by T. S. Sullivant in *Life*, circa 1921.

> Better to sing this sort of thing,
>   Heedless of guerdon and of cester—
> Ces . . . I'm immaculate of jack,
>   Writing for *Jester.*

To show our appreciation, we tendered *Jester*'s illustrious contributors a wassail bowl and banquet at the Columbia Club's downstairs tavern, the Blue Grotto, which Frank Sullivan, describing the affair next day in the *World,* insisted on calling the Grew Blotto. It was my first meeting with F.P.A., and he seemed to be a living caricature of himself: long skinny neck, narrow shoulders that sagged almost to his waist, the beaked nose and protruding lower lip which had impelled Irvin Cobb, on seeing a stuffed moose head, to exclaim, "My God, they've shot Frank Adams." His manner was blunt and somewhat forbidding, his speech clipped; it was not until I knew him better that I recognized his brusqueness as a kind of integrity, a personal protest against overblown and flowery talk. He hated verbosity. I was with him on one occasion when a long-winded bore concluded an interminable anecdote with the cliché, "Well, to make a long story short —" "Too late," F.P.A. said tersely.

Franklin Pierce Adams (the formidable array of presidential surnames was usually reduced to initials) had started as a newspaper columnist in Chicago, like his celebrated fellow townsmen Eugene Field and Bert Leston Taylor, and in 1904 he brought his column to New York under the title "Always in Good Humor," which he changed, for the better, to "The Conning Tower." It was distinguished from the outset by its excellent typography and makeup. Adams, a natural editor, would lay out each day's column with meticulous care, indicate the type he desired, carry his copy personally down to the composing room, proofread the galleys with an eagle eye for any errors.

By the Twenties he had become the leading arbiter of public opinion, the autocrat of New York's breakfast table. His style was concise, his taste flawless, his comments penetrating and to the point. He waged a ceaseless crusade against grammatical slips such as "who" for "whom" (his other noted campaigns were against invisible house numbers and dry-sweeping) and was as stalwart a champion of proper English usage as H. L. Mencken and, in subsequent years, E. B. White. He was outspoken, sometimes rude and tactless, but always honest. Once a group at The Players was denouncing a fellow clubman disliked for his boorish behavior. One member rose to his defense. "After all," he argued, "he's his own worst enemy." "Not while I'm around," Adams snapped.

The most popular feature of "The Conning Tower," and one which Adams admitted to me was his own favorite, was a weekly journal called "Diary of Our Own Mr. Pepys." In perfect parody of Samuel Pepys's seventeenth-century style, he recorded his day-by-day experiences about town, his prejudices and enthusiasms and discoveries. "In the evening to a harlequinade," he wrote in 1922, "and laughed harder at R. Benchley's drolleries than ever I have at aught else." It was the first public recognition of Robert Benchley's "Treasurer's Report," which became a classic monologue of the theater. His column was also famed for its unpredictable puns. When a theater caught fire in the Basque province of Spain, and a number of patrons were smothered trying to crowd through the single door, Adams observed sagely, "Don't put all your Basques in one exit."

In time he built up a dependable stable of contributors, most of whom wrote under noms de plume. "Freckles" was Howard Dietz, "Ambrose Glutz" was Clarence Knapp, "Baron Ireland" was Nate Salsbury, "Smeed" was Deems Taylor, "Flaccus" was Newman Levy. Each year Adams gave a dinner, at which the contributor who had placed the largest number of verses or prose bits in his column received a gold watch. (Once Adams was asked why he gave a prize for the most contributions, rather than the best one, and he threw back his head and shut his eyes for a moment in his usual attitude of thought, and then replied, "There is no such thing as the 'best' contribution. The fact that any contribution is accepted by me means that it is peerless.") There was no other remuneration; but his contributors cared no tittle for emoluments and returns. To be mentioned in "The Conning Tower" was reward enough.

His use of contributions served to keep hope alive in the hearts of a number of aspiring young writers. E. B. White, who had nothing but rejections from magazines at the outset of his career, found a haven for his work in F.P.A.'s column in the *World*. He recalled later "those tense midnights when I would approach a newsstand on Broadway and squander a nickel on the early edition to turn with secret torment of suspense to 'The Conning Tower' to discover whether some noble nubbin of poetry had achieved the decent fame I hoped it deserved." Adams ran James Thurber's first published piece in 1926, a story of Hero and Leander told in newspaper headlines, which filled an entire column of "The Conning Tower." When F.P.A. printed a comic poem of mine, during my junior year, the news made the front page of the campus paper.

That year I secured a position as Columbia correspondent with the New York *Times,* to help pay my expenses at college, but I'm afraid the *Times* did not get its twelve-dollars-a-week's worth. I was far too busy writing on my own. In addition to running the *Jester,* I had appointed myself its drama critic, an enviable position, since I received free review tickets to all the Broadway plays. Thus it became my critical lot to pass judgment on the annual Columbia Varsity Show, written and composed by three classmates of mine. I panned it unmercifully and, with rare critical foresight, predicted that its creators would never be heard from again. The book was by Oscar Hammerstein II, the lyrics by Lorenz Hart, and the musical score by Richard Rodgers.

I had bragged rashly in my review that I could do a better job myself, and accordingly I was challenged to write the book and lyrics of the 1923 Varsity Show. "Half Moon Inn," with music by Roy Webb and Morris Watkins, played a week at the Astor Hotel on Broadway, and the downtown critics were far kinder than I had been to its predecessor. At about that time, the Alumni Federation was offering a prize for a Columbia football song, so I concocted new words for the final chorus of the show and sent the entry in. The whole thing slipped my mind until the telephone at the fraternity house rang one midnight, and the irate editor of the *Times* roared, "I thought you were supposed to be our Columbia correspondent. We've just had a dispatch giving the results of their Alumni Federation song contest." I told him I hadn't heard anything about it. "Well, go out and interview the winner. His name is —" A slight pause. "Goddamit, it's you." And that was how I learned that "Roar, Lion, Roar" had won the prize.

If I was neglecting my duties with the *Times,* I displayed an even greater disregard for my studies. I was taking a course in eighteenth-century literature with Professor Harrison Ross Steeves; but I was so involved with extracurricular activities that I failed to crack a book, and had to skip the examination. Professor Steeves kindly arranged for me to take an oral test in his office a week later, but once again I was too busy to do any reading, and arrived at his office totally unprepared but resolved to bluff it through somehow. Professor Steeves was tall and saturnine — he reminded me of the conventional picture of Sherlock Holmes — with a keen sense of humor which showed in his veiled blue eyes and quizzical half-smile. When he asked

me the first question about Smollett's *Peregrine Pickle,* and I
identified the leading character as female, he ended his examination abruptly and leaned back and regarded me for a thoughtful moment. "Mr. Ford," he said, "it is quite obvious that you
are not interested in eighteenth-century writers. Perhaps this
would interest you more." He took a book from the shelf
behind him and handed it to me. "Have you ever read Max
Beerbohm's *A Christmas Garland?* Take it home with you.
We'll call it C for the course." That was my introduction to
Beerbohm's parodies; and I think Professor Steeves's amused
understanding had as much as anything to do with my becoming a literary satirist.

I had another professor at Columbia who was less understanding, but who had his inadvertent share in furthering my
career. I had signed up for a senior course in creative writing
with John Erskine, a Tennysonian figure who seemed to me
quite devoid of humor, and who read aloud the compositions of
the class in a sonorous voice which usually put me to sleep. The
composition chosen for one session was a labored and self-
conscious account of slum life, full of mildewed walls and
clogged plumbing and rats; but Erskine praised it as a work of
great art and insisted on reading every last word to us. For my
own composition the following week, I submitted a parody of
this work of great art, which annoyed Erskine so much that he
gave me a flat F and called it "an example of undergraduate
impertinence." I mentioned the incident to Professor Steeves,
and he suggested with that familiar small smile, "Why don't
you submit it to *Life?*" It was my first published article, and I
had the satisfaction of waving the check under Erskine's nose.
On the other hand, he had the satisfaction of flunking me in the
course.

During my final year at Columbia I turned out several
burlesques of the old Rover Boys books, which had been my

childhood favorites, and they amused the *Jester* readers. They seemed to amuse other readers as well, for I was invited by the editor of *Life* to write a series of Rover Boys parodies for his magazine. And so, at the tender age of twenty-one, I graduated (without a degree) into the professional world.

# 3

## *The Best Years of* Life

*L ife* today is a colossal enterprise, with a world-wide staff
running into the thousands and sumptuous home offices
sprawled over five floors of the glass-and-steel Time-Life
Building. Nothing remains of the former magazine which
Henry Luce purchased in 1936 except its name; but a few
diehards still remember with affection the old *Life* — the short
but merry one — which was the leading humor magazine of
the early Twenties.

Its staff numbered barely a dozen, and its modest editorial
sanctum took up half of one floor in an anonymous office
building at 598 Madison Avenue. A hopeful contributor would
step from the elevator into a drab reception hall, hung with
Maxfield Parrish originals and dominated by an enormous
stained-glass rendition of the traditional editorial page drawing — a mounted knight, his shield labeled LIFE and his pen
leveled like a lance, pursuing a bat-winged devil across the
landscape — which had decorated every issue since the first in
1883. The receptionist's desk was usually vacant, and after
shifting uncertainly from one foot to the other the visitor would
push open a door marked "Editorial" and enter timidly, his
precious manuscript or cartoon in hand.

And I would give all the glossy issues of Mr. Luce's *Life* to enter that door again, to breathe the familiar musty odor of cigarette smoke and printer's ink and paste, to hear the clacking typewriters and an occasional bellow from the region of the art department, to catch a glimpse of Bob Sherwood's lanky figure towering above the half-partition which fenced off the editor's private lair. The all too small office space was subdivided into smaller cubicles, desks were piled high with manuscripts and exchange magazines, everything was as cluttered and happy as a child's playroom.

*Life* was entering its best years. Charles Dana Gibson had bought it in 1920, and Robert E. Sherwood, who was promoted to editor in 1924, was rapidly lifting it out of its stodgy middle-aged rut. Gibson was as square-jawed and austere as the bust of a Roman senator; he had married one of the beautiful Langhorne sisters of Virginia, and used her as model for the famous Gibson Girl he created in the Nineties. He took no interest in the problems of advertising and circulation, and preferred to sit at his drawing board sketching a center spread for the next issue. The direction of the magazine was left to Sherwood and the art editor, bald pipe-smoking Frank Casey, whose bland Irish smile could assuage the pain of a refusal. Casey hovered over his brood of artists like a motherly hen, and there were always two or three noted illustrators perched on radiators or stacks of books in his cramped office: James Montgomery Flagg, or Ellison Hoover, or Tony Sarg, or Reginald Birch, or the white-bearded patriarchal T. S. Sullivant, or Percy Crosby, whose tough little gamin had just been christened Skippy and made a regular cartoon feature.

Sherwood was an immensely sympathetic and friendly man, slow-spoken, somber in appearance, and somewhat shy. In addition to his duties as editor, he wrote a weekly column of movie reviews, illuminated by such pungent observations as his comment on Tom Mix: "They say he rides like part of the horse, but they don't say which part." He was particularly sensitive about his spectacular height of six feet seven inches, which was the subject of endless japes by his friends. Asked at a party how well he knew Sherwood, Robert Benchley climbed onto a chair, extended his arm aloft to its full reach, and replied, "Why, I've known him since he was *this* high." And when Sherwood missed several lunches at the Algonquin Round Table because of illness, Dorothy Parker wired him: WE'VE TURNED DOWN A VACANT STEPLADDER FOR YOU.

Veteran member of *Life*'s staff when I arrived on the scene was Oliver Herford, who had written for the magazine since its first issue and whose barbed wit had strewn its pages with victims over the years. He was a figure of fantasy, short and wispy and as gray as lint: disordered gray hair, an ill-fitting gray suit, pearl-gray spats, a monocle on a long faded ribbon. (Someone asked him once why his suits were always the same color. "Saves me a world of trouble," Herford answered. "When spring comes around, I merely write my tailor, send him a small sample of dandruff, and tell him to match it exactly.") He showed up one day wearing an outrageous gray derby, and explained that it was a whim of his wife's. Friends advised him to throw it away. "Ah, but you don't know my wife," he sighed. "She has a whim of iron."

In addition to the staff writers, Sherwood had lured to *Life* such stellar contributors as Ring Lardner, Marc Connelly, Mrs. Parker, and the incomparable Mr. Benchley, whose ready laugh filled the magazine's dingy office with sunshine. Benchley's unique gift was his ability to listen, to grin in eager anticipation as you talked, to acknowledge your banal joke with a flattering guffaw. "It doesn't matter what your yarn happens to be, or how old or how shopworn," F.P.A. commented. "Benchley will burst into laughter, and you will go away thinking that you

*Quoth a painter named Phineas Platt:*
*"When I owe for the rent of my flat*
    *I draw a giraffe*
    *Which gets a sure laugh*
*And fills a whole column at that."*

"The Space Grabber," Oliver Herford's contribution to the Columbia *Jester* Celebrities Issue.

must be a witty dog." None of his quips had the faintest tinge of malice; I don't think Bob Benchley had an enemy in the world. "Everybody wanted to be his close friend, and to be with him all the time," Frank Sullivan wrote in his introduction to a posthumous collection of Benchley's articles, "and he, kindly and gregarious man that he was, would have liked to oblige. But there simply was not enough Benchley to go around."

No other humorist, with the exception of Sullivan himself, has ever been so idolized as a craftsman, so universally loved by everyone who knew him. It must have puzzled Benchley to see a twenty-one-year-old hanging around the *Life* office, but he went out of his way to be kind to me. When I started writing regularly for the magazine in 1923, I faced what was to me a serious problem. Another writer named, by wild coincidence, Torrey Ford was contributing pieces at the same time; and I asked Mr. Benchley how to avoid confusion. He pondered a moment. "You could print your own stuff in a different color ink," he suggested gravely, "but that might run into expense. Maybe the best idea would be to let Torrey handle the articles, and you handle the checks."

The building in which *Life* was located stood on the northwest corner of Madison and Fifty-ninth Street. A bank occupied the ground floor (have you ever heard of a bank on the second floor, by the way?) with a burly uniformed guard at the entrance; and Mr. Benchley, on his way to the office, had to run the gauntlet of the guard's suspicious gaze. Benchley was one of those timid souls who invariably look guilty whenever they encounter someone in uniform, whether policeman or bus driver or even Western Union messenger; but he felt that this daily scrutiny called for some overt act. Emerging from the building one afternoon, he loitered at the corner and glanced furtively up and down the street until he caught the attention of the scowling guard. In his stealthiest manner, he tore a page from his newspaper, crumpled it into a ball, knelt, and placed it against the marble side of the bank. The guard's scowl deepened and he took a menacing step forward. Hastily Benchley struck a match, lit the paper, and bolted around the corner and down Fifty-ninth Street out of sight.

Banks and Benchley never got along very well together. His persistent habit of overdrawing his account led to a certain coolness in their relationship, and staid bankers were baffled by the gay little messages he wrote when he endorsed the back of a check: "Dear Banker's Trust, I love you. Bob" or "Having wonderful time, wish you were here. Robert Rabbit Benchley." Once, when living in Crestwood, he asked his local bank for a loan, and it was given to him without question. After brooding about it overnight, he withdrew all his savings in the morning. "I don't trust a bank," he explained, "that would lend money to such a poor risk."

His casual attitude toward money was a matter of concern to all his friends. Despite the lucrative earnings from his humor articles, his radio and theater engagements, and later his phe-nomenally successful movie shorts — *How to Sleep* won the Academy Award for 1936 — he was never quite solvent. Chance acquaintances were always hitting him up for something to tide them over, he was a ready sucker for any hard-luck story along Broadway, and he had an irresistible compulsion to grab every restaurant check and bar tab. When Irving Berlin hired him to deliver his "Treasurer's Report" at the Music Box Revue, he earned five hundred dollars a week during the show's nine-month run; but after it closed he had to ask *Life* for a month's advance salary to pay his debts.

Not that he ever regretted a penny he squandered. "I am known as a bad business man from one end of the country to just a little beyond the same end," he wrote of himself frankly in 1930. "Of course, if I wanted to, I might point out that out of a possible $5000 which I have made since I left school I have had $3000 worth of good food (all of which has gone into making bone and muscle and some nice fat), $1500 worth of theater tickets, and $500 worth of candy; whereas many of my business friends have simply had $5000 worth of whatever that stock was which got so yellow along about last November."

Robert Benchley looked precisely as Gluyas Williams drew him. A master artist whose deft pen-strokes caught the plaintive and frustrated character of his subject, Williams illustrated every one of Benchley's books, and their collaboration was made in heaven. The familiar Williams portrait — round bewildered face, toothbrush mustache, a figure that tended to bulge in odd places — became Benchley's public image, and readers could visualize the dapper boulevardier whose dress shirt insisted on buckling, the hapless victim of his own bumbling inefficiency, and identify themselves with him in his bewilderment.

Since most of Benchley's articles were written in the first person, with himself the butt of his own jokes, he remains the best authority on his appearance, a subject on which he dwelt frequently. "This does not mean I am *pleased* with it, mind you, or that I can even tolerate it," he noted in an essay entitled "My Face." "I simply have a morbid interest in it." His trouble, he conceded, was that he never knew whom he would resemble in the morning until he glanced at his reflection in the mirror.

One day I look like Wimpy, the hamburger fancier in the Popeye the Sailor saga. Another day it may be Wallace Beery. And a third day, if I have let my moustache get out of hand, it is Bairnsfather's Old Bill. Some mornings, if I look in the mirror soon enough after getting out of bed, there is no resemblance to any character at all, either in or out of fiction, and I turn quickly to look behind me, convinced that a stranger has spent the night with me and is peering over my shoulder in a sinister fashion, merely to frighten me. On such occasions, the shock of finding that I am actually the possessor of the face in the mirror is sufficient to send me scurrying back to bed, completely unnerved.

Mirrors were a perpetual source of chagrin to Benchley, and he tried not to look into them any more than was absolutely necessary. "Things are depressing enough as they are," he confessed in "Malignant Mirrors," "without my going out of my way to make myself miserable." He found this particularly true when trying on a hat.

I have never seen a meaner face than mine in the hat-store mirror. I could stand its not being handsome, I could even stand looking weak in an attractive, man-about-town sort of way. But in the right-hand mirror there confronts me a hang-dog face, the face of a yellow craven, while at the left leers an even more repulsive type, sensual and cruel. Furthermore, even though I have had a haircut that very day, there is an unkempt fringe showing over my collar in back, and the collar itself (a Wimpet, 14½, which looked so well on the young man in the car-card) seems to be something which would be worn by a Maine guide when he goes into Portland for the day. My suit needs pressing and there is a general air of its having been given to me, with ten dollars, by the State on my departure from Sing Sing the day before.

Benchley lived his life in a constant state of humiliation, the prey of shoelaces that broke at inconvenient moments, fountain pens that refused to write, or military brushes that would fly out of his hands, execute a takeoff of perhaps a foot and a half, and then crash onto his forehead. "I have placed slippers very carefully under my bed," he complained, "only to have them crawl out during the night to a position where I will step into them the wrong way round when leaping out of bed to answer the telephone." He saw it as a deliberate campaign against him by the inanimate underworld. "These things don't just happen,

*I have placed slippers very carefully under my bed, only to have them crawl out during the night to a position where I will step into them the wrong way round.*

Robert Benchley, as depicted by Gluyas Williams. From
*The Benchley Roundup.*

you know. They are proofs of a very clear conspiracy to hurt me physically which exists among household objects, and against which I have no defense. All that I can do is to walk around all day crouched over with one elbow raised to ward off the heavier attacks which are being aimed at me. This gives a man a cringing look which becomes a personal characteristic."

Although Benchley has been hailed as America's greatest humorist of the century — "He wrote some of the funniest things ever written by an American," Marc Connelly stated, and Stephen Leacock agreed: "As a writer of nonsense for nonsense' sake, he is unsurpassed" — Benchley held his talents in low esteem. "It took me all these years to find I had no gift for writing," he confided to Connelly once. If someone complimented him on his style, he would protest, "I don't know enough words to have a style. I know, at the most, fifteen adjectives." He looked on himself as an amateur; and that may account for his lack of affectation, the essentially modest quality of his work.

His style was deceptively easy, but I hate to contemplate the number of embryo humorists who have come a cropper trying to imitate it. He would disarm the reader with an offhand opening paragraph: "Two or three fishermen have written in asking this department if it believes that dreams go by opposites. I am still trying to tie up their question in some way with fishing, but I can't quite figure it out. I don't even know that they were fishermen." Sometimes he would double back on his tracks and contradict his whole premise. "A great many people have come up to me and asked me how I manage to get so much work done and still keep looking so dissipated. My answer is 'Don't you wish you knew?' and a pretty good answer it is, too, when you consider that nine times out of ten I didn't hear the original question."

Benchley himself defined humor as "anything that makes anybody laugh. Personally I like humor that has extravagance, a mad quality." This quality of madness — what Joseph Bryan III has called "his dislocated logic, his combination of nonsense and *nonsequitur*" — puts him in a class with Lardner or Lear or Lewis Carroll. He had a sure ear for the absurd, as shown in his names for flowers — "double-gaited wertroot" and "Walmsley's cowlick" and "Crazy Kitty, or MacNerty's fields-awash" — or his description of a woman's dream (Case B) in "Do Dreams Go by Opposites?":

In her dream she was in a greenhouse full of exotic plants, which was on a sort of funicular, running up and down the side of a mountain. The mountain was just a shade narrower than the greenhouse, so the ends of the greenhouse jutted out on either side, making it difficult for automobile traffic, which was very heavy at this point, to pass. In the greenhouse with the woman was a deaf elk which had got in somehow through a hole in the screen. The elk couldn't hear a word that the woman was saying, so she just went on with her tapestry-weaving, as she had to have the job finished before the greenhouse got to the top of the mountain on its 11 o'clock trip. (That is, 11 o'clock from the foot of East Fourteenth Street, where it started.)

Nor could anyone else but Benchley have written:

A dog teaches a boy fidelity, perseverance and to turn around three times before lying down.

Here the matter stands, or rather *there* (it was here a minute ago).

The rooster is an entirely different sort of bird from the hen. He is very proud and has a red crest on top of his head. This red crest is put there by Nature so that the hen can see the rooster coming in a crowd and can hop into a taxi or make a previous engagement if she wants to. A favorite dodge of a lot of hens when they see the red crest of the rooster making in their direction across the barnyard is to work up a sick headache. One of the happiest and most contented roosters I ever saw was one who had had his red crest chewed off in a fight with a dog. He also wore sneakers.

Probably the best known of all Benchley classics is his 1185-word monologue called "The Treasurer's Report." Benchley is said to have composed it in eight and a half minutes on his way downtown in a taxi (considerably less time than Lincoln required for his "Gettysburg Address") and delivered it at an amateur revue put on by the group of artists and writers who lunched regularly at the Algonquin. The show was called *No, Sirree!,* after the current hit *Chauve-Souris,* and it opened — and closed — on April 30, 1922. Benchley's skit was not listed on the program, and few of the fashionable audience knew him when he walked on stage, unannounced, and began apologetically: "I shall take but a very few minutes of your time this evening, for I realize that you would much rather be listening to this interesting entertainment than to a dry financial statement."

Some of the audience glanced at their watches and looked toward the exits, and one or two at the rear of the theater left their seats and started up the aisle.

"But I *am* reminded of a story — which you have probably all of you heard," Benchley floundered. "It seems there were two Irishmen walking down the street when they came to a — Oh, I should have said in the first place that the parrot which was hanging out in *front* of the store — or rather belonging to one of these two fellows — the *first* Irishman, that is — was — well, *any*way, this parrot—"

There was a snicker in the audience, a sudden snort, a rising crescendo of laughter as it dawned on his listeners that this was a parody of the sincere but inept public speaker, caught up in the spell of his own oratory. Realizing that his story was as good as lost, Benchley abandoned it and stepped forward with a brisk businesslike air.

"Now, in connection with reading this report, there are one or two points which Dr. Murnie wanted brought up in connection with it, and he has asked me to bring them up in connec — to bring them up." Benchley made a nervous attempt to straighten his black bow tie. "In the first place, there is the question of the work which we are trying to do up there at our little place at Silver Lake, a work which we feel not only fills a very definite need in the community but also fills a very definite need — er — in the community." He gave another tug at his bow tie, which came undone. "For instance, I don't think it is generally known that most of our boys are between the age of fourteen."

The laughter had built to a steady roar, the members of the audience were doubled over holding their sides and gasping for breath, and by the time Benchley exited, bumping into the proscenium, he had already won his niche in the humorists' hall of fame.

Benchley never wanted to be known as a humorist. When he graduated from Harvard in 1912, where he earned a considerable reputation for comedy as president of the *Lampoon,* he resolved, "I'm not going to be a funny man all my life." Nathaniel Benchley, in his affectionate biography of his father, states that Benchley's private ambitions were to be a social-service worker, and to write a history of Queen Anne. Up to the time of his death, he was still collecting books on the Queen Anne period to use in the research for his magnum opus.

After college Benchley ran swiftly through a series of jobs, ranging from a brief stint organizing clambakes for the employees of a Boston paper company — "I've never looked a clam in the face since," he observed — to an even briefer engagement with the advertising department of the Curtis Publishing Company in Philadelphia. Their association terminated abruptly when Benchley, dressed in a red wig and matching beard and posing as the president of a non-existent Seattle advertising agency, delivered a lengthy diatribe against the Curtis Publishing Company at their annual banquet. He recalled later: "When I left Curtis (I was given plenty of time to get my hat and coat) I was advised not to stick to advertising. They said I was too tall, or something. I forget just what the reason was they gave." Starvation was narrowly averted when Frank Crowninshield, editor of the elite *Vanity Fair,* hired him as its managing editor at the munificent stipend of a hundred dollars a week.

Here he formed two enduring friendships: Mrs. Dorothy Parker, a demure little lady with the tongue of an adder, who was *Vanity Fair*'s drama critic, and a long lean veteran of the Canadian Black Watch named Robert E. Sherwood, its photography editor. Mrs. Parker's reviews were notoriously caustic, but when she wrote that Billie Burke "plays her lighter scenes rather as if she were giving an impression of Eva Tanguay," Miss Burke's husband Florenz Ziegfeld notified *Vanity Fair* that the magazine could choose between his advertising and Mrs. Parker's services. On the day she was fired, Sherwood and Benchley resigned in protest. Benchley's job had lasted almost nine months. "I was getting in a rut," he shrugged.

Now he found himself once more facing the problem of eking out a living. He and Mrs. Parker rented a joint office in the shabby old Metropolitan Opera House building, a secret retreat so tiny that Benchley remarked, "If it were any smaller, it would have constituted adultery." Legend has it that they printed a sign on the door: UTICA DROP FORGE & TOOL COMPANY, ROBERT BENCHLEY, PRESIDENT. DOROTHY PARKER, PRESIDENT and worked out the cable address of "Park-bench." Legend adds that day after day they sat at their respective tpewriters in unbroken seclusion until Mrs. Parker, restless for company, suggested that the door sign should be changed to read: MEN.

Robert Sherwood had been hired as movie critic of *Life,* and

Benchley, whose previous contributions had been summarily rejected by that magazine, was suddenly invited to become its drama reviewer. It was a job for which he was admirably suited. He loved the theater, and his criticisms were good-natured and gentle. If the play amused him, his infectious belly laugh could be heard throughout the theater — Brooks Atkinson remembers that "Benchley exploded like a dynamite pit" — and the delighted cast did not have to wait for his printed judgment. If he were bored, an instinctive courtesy kept him from betraying his feelings.

Only once did Benchley's good nature desert him. In May of 1922 a play by Anne Nichols, called *Abie's Irish Rose,* opened at the Fulton, the evening after a dismal flop called *The Rotters,* which Benchley described in *Life* as "the worst play of the season." Upon seeing Miss Nichols's effort, he added: "On the night following the presentation of 'The Rotters,' residents of Broadway, New York City, were startled by the sound of horses' hoofs clattering up the famous thoroughfare. Rushing to their windows, they saw a man, in Colonial costume, riding a bay mare from whose eyes flashed fire. The man was shouting as he rode, and his message was: ' "The Rotters" is no longer the worst play in town: "Abie's Irish Rose" has just opened!' "

Unfortunately Benchley had established the custom of following his weekly criticism with brief summaries of previous reviews, called "Confidential Guide," which he rewrote for each successive issue; and as *Abie's Irish Rose* continued to flourish month after month, despite its negative notices, Benchley found himself hard put to invent new ways of saying "Among the season's worst" or "Something awful." His frantic struggles to improvise became a public joke: People bought *Life* just to read such efforts at evasion as "There is no letter W in the French alphabet" or "Flying fish are sometimes seen at as great a height as fifteen feet" or "Will the Marines *never* come?" When the cast of *Abie* sent him a derisive birthday cake on the first anniversary of its spectacular run, he noted feebly: "To be reviewed next week." The play set a Broadway record of 2327 performances, and by the fifth year Benchley was reduced to holding a prize contest for suggestions. Harpo Marx won with "No worse than a bad cold."

Frank Sullivan voiced the feelings of Benchley's innumerable friends after his untimely death in 1945: "Just to meet him and say Hello was a tonic. For my own selfish part, I give thanks that he lived in this age, for that happy circumstance enabled me to have the rich, joyous, and rewarding experience of knowing him, and delighting in him."

I never really knew Ring Lardner; a mere handful of people knew him well. He visited the *Life* office only once that I remember, in the fall of 1924, when he brought in the manuscript of one of his burlesque surrealist dramas called "Clemo Uti — 'The Water Lilies.' " Sherwood introduced me to him; but since Lardner seldom spoke, and I was too awed to say anything, our conversation consisted of a couple of grave nods. Even that brief and wordless encounter left an indelible impression. He was the most completely silent man I have ever met, solemn and unsmiling and yet curiously appealing. His face was gaunt, with high cheekbones and shadowy hollows — someone compared his vaulted features to a cathedral — and reminded me in an odd way of Buster Keaton. Like Keaton, the mournful expression gave his comedy an incongruous and eerie value. The dark melancholy eyes were extraordinarily sensitive. As Scott Fitzgerald said, "A noble dignity flowed from him."

Although ill-at-ease and silent in the presence of strangers, he would sit up all night talking with his intimates. John Wheeler, his close friend and syndicate manager for many years, wrote that "he could be the most droll and convivial of companions. To be accepted by him was to enter a magic circle of camaraderie." One of his early jobs, before becoming a journalist, had been with a firm which collected bad debts. "I never heard of a good debt," he observed to Wheeler later. His wit was always trenchant and fresh. Once he declined a dinner invitation with the brief telegram: THIS IS THE CHILDREN'S NIGHT OUT, AND I HAVE TO STAY HOME WITH THE NURSE. When his sons were attending the best prep schools, Wheeler recalls, he used to refer to them as his four grandsons "because they cost me four grand a year."

Lardner had an uncanny ability to catch the American idiom, and his "Alibi Ike" stories, based on a rookie pitcher he had known when he was a Chicago sportswriter, introduced such oft-imitated phrases as "further and more" or "and etc." He was a savage social satirist, flensing human selfishness and cruelty in his masterly short stories, "Haircut" and "Golden Honeymoon," which have been compared to the best of de Maupassant and Chekhov. The British critic William Bolitho called him "the greatest and sincerest pessimist America has produced." Even his humor had an owlish quality: the sober misuse of a word — " 'Shut up,' he explained" — or the dead-pan dialogue of his expressionist drama, "I Gaspiri — 'The Upholsterers,' " a Lardner classic:

### Characters

Ian Obri, a Blotter Salesman.
Johan Wasper, his wife.
Herbert Swope, a nonentity.
Ffena, their daughter, later their wife.
Egso, a Pencil Guster.
Tono, a Typical Wastebasket.

(Translator's Note: *This show was written as if people were there to see it.*)

## ACT I

(*A public street in a bathroom. A man named Tupper has evidently just taken a bath. A man named Brindle is now taking a bath. A man named Newburn comes out of the faucet which has been left running. He exits through the exhaust. Two strangers to each other meet on the bath mat.*)

FIRST STRANGER

Where was you born?

SECOND STRANGER

Out of wedlock.

FIRST STRANGER

That's a mighty pretty country around there.
(*The curtain is lowered for seven days to denote the lapse of a week.*)


## ACT III

(*The Lincoln Highway. Two bearded glue lifters are seated at one side of the road.*)

FIRST GLUE LIFTER

Well, my man, how goes it?

SECOND GLUE LIFTER

(*Sings "My Man" to show how it goes.*)

## CURTAIN


Ring Lardner's last piece — he died in 1933 in his latter forties — was written in the hospital while he was mortally ill. "Odd's Bodkins" was a superb parody of O. O. ("Odd") McIntyre's name-dropping newspaper column, and Lardner, who loved best writing lyrics, led off with a brief poem of explanation:

Each morn when the neighbors are through with our papers
And stealthily slide them beneath our front door,
I grab the *American,* knowing that there I can
Find O. O. McIntyre's column of lore.
You ask what it's like? I've no copy right here,
But p'rhaps I can give you some sort of idear.

*Diary of a Modern New Yorker:* Up and out five hours before dawn,
and by scooter to the Hermitage Hotel, where the big Seminole
Indian chief, Gwladys, cooked me a flagon of my favorite breakfast
dish, beet root and wrestlers' knees . . . Home for a moment to slit
my mail, and found invitations from Mussolini, Joan Blondell, Joan
Crawford, Joan of Arc, President Buchanan, Joe Walcott, and Louisa
M. Alcott.

*Thingumbobs:* If they did not wear identical hats, Jack Dempsey and
Connie Bennett could easily pass for sisters . . . One word description of Franklin Delano Roosevelt — President . . . There is something about the name Babe Ruth that suggests rare old Dresden
filigree work . . . Tallulah Bankhead and Jimmy Durante have
profiles exactly alike . . .

*Thoughts While Strolling:* Damon Runyon's feet. Kate Smith, a
small-town girl who became nationwide in a big city. Rosamund
Pinchot and Theodore Dreiser could pass for twins. Rube Goldberg
never wears a hat to bed. There is a striking resemblance between
Damon Runyon's feet and Ethel Merman . . .

"Lardner had an ear for the dim sad music of America that
nobody else could touch," E. B. White wrote in his "Notes and
Comments" in *The New Yorker.* "The funnier his stuff was,
the more deadly the aim. 'Odd's Bodkins' happens to be a good
example of Lardner; but if it were below par it would still be
better than most anybody else's masterpiece."

*Life* in the early Twenties — and it was as true of the period
as of the magazine — was tranquil and unconcerned with

change. The standard he-he, she-she, and he-she jokes still appeared under its cartoons (Harold Ross's *New Yorker,* yet unborn, was the first to reduce a caption to one line or none at all) and the magazine went in heavily for prize contests ("$500 for the best title to this picture") and charity drives to raise money for rebuilding the Louvain Library, or to establish an annual Fresh Air Fund for slum children. Its weekly editorials by E. S. Martin were amiable and aimless, its political cartoons by C. B. Sykes innocuous to the point of being insipid: a genial Uncle Sam remonstrating with John Bull about the British war debt; a comic figure labeled "Coal Shortage" popping up out of a jack-in-the-box; a pirate's ghost, complete with wooden leg and earrings, saluting some modern rum runners; a buxom angel laying a wreath on the coffin of Warren Gamaliel Harding ("The most notable quality in Mr. Harding was the sweetness of his nature," Martin eulogized. "He gave out love, and . . . love is the greatest thing in the world"). There was little or no capacity for outrage; the public looked on issues like Prohibition or Teapot Dome with a cynical indifference, and did not want to be jolted out of its complacency.

My Rover Boys parodies seemed to fit this mood. No national problems were involved; they were pure and simple spoofs of those durable boyhood favorites by Arthur M. Winfield (the nom de plume of Edward Stratemeyer, also author of *The Motor Boys* and other juvenile epics) who had created the Rover Boys during the Spanish-American War and had kept them at Putnam Hall ever since. After a couple of my parodies had appeared in *Life,* Robert Sherwood decided to break the magazine's routine with a ten-part serial. In May of 1925, *Life* announced that the following week's issue would inaugurate "The Rover and Over Boys, a thrilling serial of Love and Adventure, with illustrations by Gluyas Williams. The pranks of these fun-loving lads have thrilled millions of readers

door. "1812, the war of," Sherwood said ominously, and w
knocked and entered. The white-haired creator of the Rove
Boys was seated behind a bare desk, his eyes glinting behin
steel-rimmed spectacles, his face contorted with anger. Befor
we could utter a word, he embarked on a tirade, accusing us o
stealing his characters and using them without permission.
tried to point out that the articles in *Life* were intended a
parodies. "Making fun of my books?" he bellowed, poundin;
his fist, "That's even worse!" It took all of Sherwood's diplo
macy to calm him; and we finally agreed that the names of th
trio would be changed henceforth to "The Rollo Boys," and
*Life* would publish an abject apology together with a persona
letter from Mr. Stratemeyer. The letter was far funnier than
anything in the series:

How did I come to write The Rover Boys' stories, and how did I
happen to pick out the pen name of Arthur M. Winfield? Well, for
a long time I had had in mind to write a series dealing with up-to-
date American boys. Many of our books of those days had an English
setting, or else were of the wishy-washy Sunday school volume type.
I remembered that when I had gone to Sunday school we had a library
of over a thousand volumes, and of those the boys did not care for
more than a dozen. And at the public library, a small affair, we were
handed dilapidated copies of "The Water Babies" or "Deeds of
Daring Travelers," the latter with little woodcuts of lions, snakes,
and the like. I wrote the first three volumes of The Rover Boys one
summer, and I have been writing one volume a year ever since.

Now as to the pen name, Arthur M. Winfield. One evening, when
writing with my mother sitting near sewing, I remarked that I
wanted an assumed name — that I wasn't going to use my own name
on the manuscript I was then turning out, a short story for a
religious weekly. She thought a moment and suggested Winfield.
"For then," she said, "you may win in that field." I thought that
good and then asked about a front name. "Well," she said, "if you

throughout a series of volumes which, if laid end to end, would
stretch. Follow the Rover Boys around the world! They are true-
blue and American to the core! A trial subscription entered NOW
will bring you the entire series."

The first installment, entitled "A Crew Race and What
Followed (Besides the Other Crew)," occupied a two-page
spread, with gorgeous drawings by Williams and a tactful
editorial bow to the late Mr. Stratemeyer. I quote the opening
dialogue, with some embarrassment, as evidence of how easy it
was to make people laugh in those days:

"Quick, Tom!" cried a brown-eyed, curly-haired youth of nineteen
as he grabbed up an oar and started toward the river. "Where is
Sam?"

"Here I am," replied a tall serious youth, seizing another oar and
following his brother. "Where is Dick?"

"Here I am, too," answered a sturdy youth of eighteen summers,
selecting a third oar which he had carefully feathered the night
before in preparation for the great race today with Rival Academy,
"and that was Sam who spoke first."

"No, it wasn't," interrupted the tall, serious youth. "It was Dick.
This is Sam speaking now."

"No, this one *here* is Sam," insisted the sturdy youth of eighteen
summers. "You are Dick yourself. As a matter of fact, it was Tom
who spoke first, because he is the brown-haired, curly-eyed Rover
Boy, and full of mischief."

"Three rousing cheers for the Rover Boys!" shouted the cadets in
perfect unison. "Suffice it to say for the benefit of those who have not
read the 397 previous volumes of the Rover Boys Series for Young
Americans — " and here the students glared suspiciously at one
another — "suffice it to say that they are red-blooded 100% American
he-boys, and since they came to Putnam Hall a quarter of a century
ago they have had numerous adventures, so many in fact that they can
scarcely be hinted at here, as related in full in the list on the back

cover, for all our young readers from sixteen to sixty provided there *are* that many. Hurray! hurray! hurray!"

This was followed by a succession of Tom Rover's fun-loving pranks involving collapsible chairs and loaded cigars ("Tom was much sought after, sometimes with rifles") until the crew race was won, Dan Baxter and Mumps the toady were thrown into a quandary with steep slippery sides, and the happy though hoarse students of Putnam Hall called for a final cheer, leading to the invariable concluding paragraph:

The cheers were given with a will; but the contents of that will, and how it affected the fortunes of our young heroes, will be related in the next volume of this fascinating series to be entitled: "The Rover Boys in Florida; or, How Tom Found Lots Under Water." And here let us say good-by.

*Good-by.*

"The Rover and Over Boys" had reached its eighth install-ment, John Farrar of *The Bookman* had engaged me to do another series of parodies to be called "The Rover Boys in Literature," and the George H. Doran Company had contracted to publish the whole collection that fall under the title *Three Rousing Cheers;* when suddenly the boom descended. It turned out that the late Edward Stratemeyer was still very much alive. Not only alive, but choleric with rage and threatening to sue *Life* and myself for plagiarism. The series was promptly halted (I don't recall that any trial subscribers demanded their money back), lawyers were consulted, and Bob Sherwood and I were advised to call on Mr. Stratemeyer in person and seek to smooth matters over before the suit began.

Mr. Stratemeyer's office was in Room 1812 of the Flatiron Building, and Sherwood and I ascended in a creaky elevator, walked along several miles of corridor, and paused before the

Illustration by Gluyas Williams for *Three Rousing Cheers.* Don-ald Ogden Stewart introduces Dick, Tom, and Sam Rover to Humorists' Circle. Around the table, counterclockwise: Ir— Cobb, Marc Connelly, George S. Kaufman, Stephen Leaco— Heywood Broun, Dorothy Parker, Will Rogers, Ring Lardn— and on the floor, studying a newt, Robert Benchley.

are going to be an author, why not make it Arthur?" And so it became Arthur. And then to make it look more natural, I inserted the middle initial M, saying that M stood for thousands and it might help us to sell thousands of books.

And now I'll let you into a little secret. The original cover design, used on the first ten or twelve volumes, was my work. And there you are.

That same summer Robert Sherwood, with his flair for the unusual, recalled that while at Harvard Benchley had put out a highly successful *Lampoon* parody of *Life*. He enlisted Benchley's help, and they collaborated on a travesty of the tabloid newspaper, a phenomenon which had first appeared on the American scene six years before and had already achieved a mass circulation of better than a million. The Burlesque Number was called the *Daily Life* ("over a million readers," it claimed, "many of whom can read"), and its front page featured a sensational photograph of a "Brutal Axe-pest" (Harpo Marx) about to hack a victim (Benchley, lying prostrate with a whimpering expression) while Detective Ermbody (Sherwood) looked on nonchalantly, smoking a cigar. The issue sold out, and burlesque numbers became the new fad

Probably the most memorable was *Life*'s "News-Stand Number," on August 18, 1925, which bore a shocking cover promising "Thrills, Sensations, Confessions, and other Popular Forms of Bunk," and which scatter-gunned every current magazine from *Photoplay* to the *New Republic*. John Held and Rea Irvin and Rube Goldberg did the lurid illustrations. Herman J. Mankiewicz contributed a lampoon of the Octavus Roy Cohen stories, in which every line of dialogue was "That is just what I ain't got nothin' else but." Tip Bliss wrote "A Novel of Despair" which consisted entirely of a synopsis of previous installments; I tackled the sagebrush school of romance with

**BRUTAL** axe-pest, George LaMoll of 1367 Wheeden Ave., Queens, poses for DAILY LIFE photographer, showing how he hacked victims after knocking them down first. LaMoll, in the custody of Detective Ermbody, is shown with axe (*arrow*).

From *Life*'s "Daily Life" parody issue. Harpo Marx, Robert Sherwood, and the victim, Robert Benchley.

" 'Slim' Larabee of Tarnation Ridge" ("him with a ready trigger and a heart o' gold"), full of rough-hewn Western talk like "Drap them thar shootin' irons" or "Whut tarnation devil's mockery mought this be?"; and Dorothy Parker leveled her sights on MacFadden's *True Story* in the parody sex confession of a picture-postcard model, with the titillating subtitle: "She came to that magic Fairyland which men call BROADWAY — and was blinded by the glitter of its wickedness."

Equally devastating was Marc Connelly's Success Story called " 'I Approve of Reading,' says Joseph L. Gonnick, President of the Joseph L. Gonnick Cantilever Bridge Co." The lead photograph showed Joseph L. Gonnick (Connelly) explaining to a lady visitor (Mrs. Parker) how his employees (Marx and Sherwood) were encouraged to read good books (both men were clutching a copy of the *Saturday Evening Post*). In sly imitation of that magazine's style, Mr. Gonnick stated in the accompanying interview:

*The Saturday Evening Post* is perhaps the ideal business man's magazine. It appears on Thursday, though I have a private arrangement with my newsdealer by which I get it on Wednesday night. The characters in the stories are frankly of a manly and womanly character, quite unlike the neurotic types one finds elsewhere . . . I do not believe a man can really be a citizen of the world unless he reads a magazine like the *S. E. Post*. It is part of the staple diet in the "Gonnick Free Reading Rooms" at our Shreveport, Olean and Chicago works. I say in all seriousness that if I had not been called to the world of business instead, I should probably now be one of its writers.

High point of the "News-Stand Number," for me at least, was Robert Benchley's two-fisted and hard-hitting "Horse Sense Editorial," my favorite example of Benchley at his inimitable best:

*"Yes," said Joseph L. Gonnick* [Marc Connelly] *to a visitor* [Dorothy Parker], *"I always encourage my men* [Harpo Marx and Robert Sherwood] *to read good books."*

From *Life*'s "News-Stand" parody issue.

A man walked into my office the other day and tried to sell me some buttercups.

"Some buttercups, Mr. Blank?" he said, smiling.

"When you say that, smile," I replied. And from the way I spoke, he knew that I meant what I said.

Now that man went about his job in the wrong way. Most of us go about our jobs in the wrong way. We forget the other fellow. They say that an elephant never forgets. Did you ever hear of an elephant failing in business? Elephants never forget, and daisies won't tell. Two things that we humans might well take to heart.

Supposing Moses had forgotten the other fellow. The great Law-Giver was, above all else, a two-fisted business man. He knew the rate of exchange, and he knew that what goes up must come down. Moses was no elephant. Neither was he a daisy. And yet Moses will be remembered when most of us are forgotten.

The other day I met an old school-mate. He was crying. "Well, old timer," I said, "what's that you've got in your hand?"

"My other hand," he replied, shaking it.

Now the reason my old school-mate hadn't made good was that he kept one hand inside the other. He was drawing on his principal. He had never heard of such a thing as interest . . .

On the street in which I live there is a line of trees. They are big, fine trees, full of twigs and branches. All except one. This one tree has no twigs or branches. It hasn't even any leaves. It just stands there. One day last week I determined to see what was wrong with that tree. I wanted to know why, in a line of fine, strong trees, there should be one weak one. I suspected that it wasn't playing the game right.

So I went close to it and examined it. It wasn't a tree at all. It was a hydrant.

Watch out that you aren't a hydrant in a line of trees. Or, worse yet, a line of trees in a hydrant.

# 4

## *Taverns of the Twenties*

P ROHIBITION, which we had denounced so roundly in 1920 when it went into effect, proved to be an unexpected boon. Since nobody in the Twenties believed that the Eighteenth Amendment could ever be repealed, people adjusted themselves to the inevitable and settled down to breaking the law as pleasantly as possible. The old saloon went underground (at least, to the basement level) and the new speakeasy, with its mixed drinks and mixed company, became the haven of a public parched as much for conviviality as for alcohol.

Drinking had never been so much fun back in the wide-open days before Volstead. Now an evening on the town involved adventure and cloak-and-dagger intrigue. Chauffeured limousines would halt before a shuttered brownstone front, and fashionable couples would descend a flight of dark stairs to the servants' entrance, blocked by a steel door. The sliding panel, the furtive inspection by unseen eyes, the chains and bolts that slid open at the magic Sesame gave a visitor the snobbish feeling of belonging to an exclusive club. There was a cozy sense of conspiracy about it all, a mutual defiance of danger — largely imaginary, since most of the speakeasies had worked out a practical arrangement with the authorities — which united the patrons against a common enemy. As a rule, the cellar space was cramped, the air foul, the bedlam of voices deafening, the lighting so dim you couldn't see what you were drinking. Which was just as well, for most of the liquor was prepared by Sicilian alky-burners and mixed with artificial flavoring and labeled Rye or Scotch or Gin, depending on the color. You had to order it shaken up in a Bronx or a Pink Lady to make it palatable; but that didn't matter. The drinking itself was incidental to the camaraderie of these welcome watering holes in Prohibition's arid desert.

New York offered them in infinite variety, ranging from the sawdust pubs along First Avenue to the ornate gin palaces of the side streets in the Fifties and Sixties. There was the Pre Catalan, probably the earliest collegiate hangout. The Bernaise with its white trellises and dusty artificial vines, its overstuffed sofas ranged along the wall, its low marble-topped tables over which the customers crouched like Neanderthal men squatting around a fire. Matt Winkle's on Park Avenue opposite the Racquet Club, so popular with the weekend campus trade that the Yale *News* and the Harvard *Crimson* ran advertisements showing the proprietor, clad in a coonskin coat and leaning against a Stutz Bearcat, with the caption: *Matt Winkle Himself.*

Some speakeasies clung stubbornly to the old tradition that a saloon should be for men only. Jack Bleeck's Artist and Writers, adjoining the *Tribune* building on West Fortieth Street, limited its clientele to masculine tipplers, mostly newspaper men. Dan and Mort Moriarty likewise refused stoutly to admit members of the opposite sex to their famed establishment at 216 East 58th Street; and indignant ladies such as Ruth Hale, wife of Heywood Broun and a dedicated Lucy Stoner, were forced to wait outside in a Yellow cab for an hour or so while their escorts tarried at Dan's bar. The Moriarty clientele was a happy blend of neighborhood Irish, apartment house doormen and janitors and police lieutenants in mufti, and what Dan called "gintlemin," dignified bankers and brokers and Yale and Princeton undergraduates, often in full evening dress. Lucius Beebe, a regular patron, recalled that there were two prices for drinks — fifty cents for the Irish and six bits for the "gintlemin." Another patron, though somewhat irregular, was Harry Gerguson, the self-styled Prince Michael Romanoff of all the Russias, who was said to have escaped deportation by swimming ashore from Ellis Island, and who was never more than one jump ahead of the immigration officers. Once the authorities cornered the fugitive at Dan's, and Mike lowered himself through a trapdoor behind the bar and hid for three days in a coal bin, subsisting on sardines and Scotch.

Most elegant and expensive of the town's bistros was Jack and Charlie's Puncheon Club at 42 West 49th Street, later moved to a swanker location at 21 West 52d Street and renamed The Iron Gate or, more simply, "21." Instead of the usual diluted grain alcohol and spiked grape juice, "21" went in for genuine imported liquors and vintage wines — even during the great drought you could obtain an authentic Clos de Vougeot, a Montrachet 1889, a Romanée-Conti 1880 — and superb food prepared by a *chef de cuisine* whose salary was reputed to be twenty thousand dollars. Under the personal supervision of Jack Kriendler and his jovial partner Charlie Berns, it was a homing point for celebrities from as far as London and Hollywood. Gathered around its red-checkered tablecloths of an evening you might find Mr. Benchley and Mrs. Parker and Harold Ross, Gene Fowler and Charlie Mac-Arthur and Ben Hecht, Nunnally Johnson, Damon Runyon, "Bugs" Baer, Howard Dietz, George Jean Nathan, Rube Goldberg, Gene Tunney, and, of course, the ubiquitous Prince Mike.

Every precaution was taken to elude the law in case of a raid.

The cellar beneath "21" and the adjoining Number 19, also owned by Jack and Charlie, was a catacomb of well-stocked wine bins, concealed behind sliding panels and sections of solid concrete wall which would swing open when a piece of wire was inserted in a crack, or when an ordinary coathanger established electric contact. There were five of these storage caches, each capable of holding five thousand cases of whiskey and wine. One night eight federal agents, armed with search warrants, invaded "21" and spent twelve hours in the downstairs labyrinth, measuring and tapping and probing in vain. "We shut off the electricity," Charlie explained later. As added insurance, the bar was hinged and in an emergency could be lowered by touching a button, dropping its bottles and glasses down a brick-lined chute to shatter against iron baffles and rocks and spill every drop of evidence into a convenient sewer drain. It was never used during Prohibition; but several days after repeal, the story goes, Jack Kriendler was showing the ingenious device to a friend during the evening rush hour. "All you have to do is press this button here," he said, and absent-mindedly pressed it, sending a small fortune in precious potables crashing onto the rocks below.

Such were the Mermaid Taverns of the Twenties, where the funnymen foregathered and laughter prospered and bon mots were bandied back and forth, to be repeated around town the next day if anyone was sober enough to remember them. Sometimes the habitués of the Puncheon Club moved across the street to Tony Soma's, which offered cheaper drinks and mediocre Italian cooking, or migrated en masse to a favorite haunt of Benchley's off Seventh Avenue which he called "that little French place completely without charm." It was at Tony's that Mr. Benchley took his first social drink. His New England upbringing had kept him a teetotaler all these years until Mrs. Parker urged him to try an Orange Blossom, just for size. He sipped, shuddered, and set down the glass. "This place ought to be closed by law," he said sternly. And it was also at Tony's that Mrs. Parker was accosted by a hearty drunk who slapped her shoulder and shouted an obscene pleasantry as he wove past the table. Mrs. Parker mopped a spilled Martini from her lap. "Just a rhinestone in the rough," she purred.

Dorothy Parker was small and attractive, with dark bobbed hair and melting eyes and the innocent mien of a schoolgirl. She seemed as demure as a kitten, but the unwary soon learned that her sheathed claws were lightning-fast and could leave a painful scratch. Alexander Woollcott called her "a blend of Little Nell and Lady Macbeth . . . She has the gentlest, most disarming demeanor of anyone I know. But Mrs. Parker carries — as everyone is uneasily aware — a dirk which knows no brother and mighty few sisters." Her deadliest comments were usually delivered in a murmured aside, while her face remained all smiles as she watched a dear friend depart: "That woman speaks eighteen languages, and can't say No in any of them." Or, when a tipsy table partner at Tony's shoved back his chair and announced in a loud voice that he had to go take a leak, Mrs. Parker apologized for him in her sweetest manner: "He really wants to telephone, but he's too embarrassed to say so."

Quoting Mrs. Parker became the town's leading indoor sport. If someone wanted to take over a dinner conversation, he had merely to say, "Did you hear Dorothy's latest?" All sorts of spurious quips were attributed to her; but the genuine coin had an unmistakable ring. As when she insisted that her dog had caught a social disease from using a public lamppost. Or when she explained that she had named her canary Onan because it scattered its seed. Again, when a real estate agent was showing her an apartment for rent. "Oh, dear, that's *much* too big," she protested. "All I need is room enough to lay a hat and a few friends."

The quotations could go on endlessly. There was the night that Mrs. Parker arrived at a Halloween party given by Herbert Bayard Swope, and inquired what the guests were doing. "They're ducking for apples," her host explained. Mrs. Parker shook her head sadly. "There, but for a typographical error," she sighed, "is the story of my life."

Her poems were exquisite cameos, poignant and haunting, but, perversely, she insisted on tripping herself up in the last line and reducing the effort to comic verse. Generally they pictured a hapless lass, the victim of unrequited love, whose golden boy goes galloping off over the horizon while she utters a final taunt: "Inseparable my nose and thumb." The disillusioned lady of the sonnets asked no sympathy, preferring to go down, as Woollcott said of Mrs. Pat Campbell once, "like a sinking ship firing on its rescuers." Her cynicism matched the mood of the times in her "Prophetic Soul":

> Because your eyes are slant and slow,
> > Because your hair is sweet to touch,
> My heart is high again; but, oh,
> > I doubt if this will get me much.

Or her oft-quoted couplet "News Item":

> Men seldom make passes
> At girls who wear glasses.

Or her rueful lament called "Theory," as lovely as anything by A. E. Housman:

> Into Love and out again,
> > Thus I went, and thus I go.
> Spare your voice, and hold your pen—
> > Well and bitterly I know

> All the songs were ever sung,
>     All the words were ever said;
> Can it be, when I was young,
>     Some one dropped me on my head?

"The humorist has never been happy," she wrote once; and it is her cross to be best known today for her tart epigrams, rather than for her poetry or her bitter and brilliant short stories. ("Big Blonde" is as corrosive as Lardner's "Haircut.") But this is the penalty she must pay for her uncanny ability to find the precise cutting word, the telling epithet. Broadway will long remember that prolonged blood bath when she substituted for Mr. Benchley as *Life*'s drama critic, and noted that "Katherine Hepburn ran the gamut of emotions from A to B." Equally scathing was her brief review of *The House Beautiful,* a tedious effort by Channing Pollock: " 'The House Beautiful' is the play lousy." Then of course there was her statistical survey of a Princeton prom: "If all the girls were laid end to end, I wouldn't be surprised." But the Parkerism I treasure most is her telegram to Bob Sherwood's diminutive wife Mary on the birth of a baby girl. For months the expectant mother had arrived at the Algonquin Round Table so ostentatiously big with child that everyone was becoming concerned about the prolonged pregnancy, and Marc Connelly, on behalf of her friends, took her aside and advised her solemnly to abandon the whole project. At last she delivered the belated offspring, and Mrs. Parker wired her: CONGRATULATIONS, DEAR, WE ALL KNEW YOU HAD IT IN YOU.

Benchley and Dorothy Parker and the Donald Ogden Stewarts were constant companions at the town taverns. Don Stewart was a newcomer out of Yale, with a broad benevolent smile and blue eyes blinking behind steel-rimmed spectacles. He had developed a wondrously funny style all his own, with a nightmare quality in which a scene would shift imperceptibly as he wrote, and the helpless reader would find himself drifting from a restaurant to a railroad train to a dentist's office, which would dissolve in turn into an ocean liner and then a Turkish bath. His genius for the absurd was revealed in the very first paragaph of the first chapter of his first book, *A Parody Outline of History*. In the rapturous manner of William Lyon Phelps, it began:

On a memorable evening in the year 1904 I witnessed the opening performance of Maude Adams in "Peter Pan." Nothing in the world can describe the tremendous enthusiasm of that night! I shall never forget the moment when Peter came to the front of the stage and asked the audience if we believed in fairies. I am happy to say that I was actually the first to respond. Leaping at once out of my seat, I shouted "Yes    Yes!" To my intense pleasure the whole house almost instantly followed my example, with the exception of one man. This man was sitting directly in front of me. His lack of enthusiasm was to me incredible. I pounded him on the back and shouted, "Great God, man, are you alive? Wake up! Hurrah for the fairies! Hurrah!" Finally he uttered a rather feeble "Hurrah!"

That was my first meeting with that admirable statesman Woodrow Wilson.

Benchley's friendship with Stewart, according to Nathaniel Benchley's biography of his father, blossomed one rainy night when they emerged from Tony's, and a sidewalk attendant hurried toward them with an open umbrella. Stewart stepped under it, took the little man's arm, and ordered, "Yale Club, please." Benchley promptly ducked under the same umbrella, grasped the man's other arm, and said to Stewart, "I'll drop you off. It's right on my way."

There was an instant telepathy between them, and the same idea would occur to them simultaneously. One afternoon they were strolling up Fifth Avenue past the Public Library, where a wooden reviewing stand still remained after yesterday's parade. Without a word, Stewart climbed to the fourth row and seated himself, and Benchley took his place before the empty stand, raised one fist like a cheerleader, and swung it downward in three successive movements. "Rah! rah! rah!" Stewart chanted, and then climbed down from the stand, and they continued serenely on their way to Tony's.

Each speakeasy had its own clientele, all members of the same secret fraternity. I more or less belonged to 109 East 61st Street, a modest basement hideout run by Jim Moriarty, younger brother of Dan and Mort, who had deserted his bartender duties at the family establishment near Third Avenue to open his own business at a more impressive address. Jim was a tall good-looking young Irishman, with social aspirations which his older brothers lacked, and he affected a carnation in his lapel and a cultivated Park Avenue accent. His place was small but tastefully decorated: rich carpeting, a leather-faced bar in the front half of the long narrow room, tables and leather chairs at the rear. Often Jim himself would peer through the peephole in the front door to identify his customers, and usher them inside with the gracious bow of a polished host.

Among the most faithful of the "109" group — everyone moved in groups in those days — were Frank Sullivan and Russel Crouse and his wife Alison Smith, who worked under Woollcott as drama page editor of the *World*. Alison was wonderful company, all animation and fun, and her contralto voice and deep guttural chuckle warmed you like an open hearth. She was also notably absentminded. After a night at "109," the bar would be strewn with personal objects she had left behind in her restless progress down its full length: one glove, a compact, her cigarette box, the other glove, her purse, and finally Alison herself perched on the last stool. She was one of those unfortunates who never remember names, but always forget a face. Shortly after she and Crouse were married, she undertook to introduce her new husband to Woollcott at a theater opening. "Alec, this is Mister —" she began, and floundered. Crouse opened his wallet and handed her a visiting card. "Crouse is the name, dear."

Her inability to recall where she put things down was a constant problem. One night Frank Sullivan called at her apartment to take her to the opera, and Alison wasted half an hour searching for her various accouterments. As they hurried out of the apartment, the door banged behind them, and she halted abruptly, a faraway expression on her face. "Frank, what's that Greek word that means the name is like the sound . . . you know . . . ominous or antimacassar or something like that?" Sullivan seized her elbow and shoved her into the elevator. "Come on, Smith, we're late." All the way down to the lobby she was in a brown study, and they rode in a taxi in total silence for several blocks until her face suddenly brightened. "Frank!" she remembered. "Onomatopoeia!"

"You should have attended to that before you left the apartment," Sullivan replied crossly.

Alison was easily moved to tears — Crouse claimed that she cried at card tricks — and was particularly emotional about Ireland. Though there was no trace of the Auld Sod in her ancestry, she would weep copiously whenever she heard an Irish lullaby, and never missed a St. Patrick's Day parade. One night on her way to "109" she discovered to her delight that the cabdriver had as rich a brogue as ever you'd be hearing in the Emerald Isle. She promptly fell in love with him, and asked sentimentally what part of Erin he came from. "Kilkenny, ma'am," he answered. Alison clasped her hands in delight. "Oh, that's where the cats do all the fighting, isn't it?" The driver turned and gave her a stern look. "An' why shouldn't they stick up for their rights?" he demanded. Alison was crushed for the rest of the ride.

Her hands were always in motion, dipping and swerving to accent what she was saying. The only trouble was that the gesture never quite matched the subject. She would form a circle with thumb and forefinger to illustrate the phrase "My mother . . ." or make a victory V as she said, "So I went upstairs . . ." or else remark, "Next summer we're going to Norway," and point vaguely in the direction of the door. Her words had a similar way of jumbling themselves. When Crouse and Lindsay's *Life with Father* opened in Washington, the cast was invited to dine with the President at the Executive Mansion, and Alison to her consternation found herself seated on the right of Franklin D. Roosevelt. Thrown into total panic by the proximity of her great idol, she made an abortive effort to start conversation. "Tell me, Mr. President," she floundered, "who was the artichoke of the White House?"

Sometimes Heywood Broun would lumber into "109" with the bogus Prince Michael Romanoff in tow. Broun was huge, slovenly in dress (intimates likened him to an unmade bed), and a stalwart champion of the downtrodden in his column in the *World* "It Seems to Me." Since no one could possibly seem more trodden down than Prince Mike, wandering from pub to pub in quest of free drinks, Broun had taken him under his capacious wing. Once Broun found his protégé seated on the curb outside "109," green-faced and doubled over with pain. Assuming that he had imbibed some rotgut whiskey in his nocturnal prowls, Broun hurried him inside, and fetched a bottle of milk for him to swallow as an antidote. Mike opened his eyes weakly, and gazed at the label. "Grade B milk for a Romanoff!" he protested in outraged pride, and flung the bottle across the room.

Marc Connelly was a frequent patron, and one afternoon at Jim's establishment marked an important point in his career. Marc had been laboring on a dramatization of Roark Bradford's *Ole Man Adam and His Chillun,* but no theatrical producer was willing to take a chance on a play about the Old Testament with an all-Negro cast. Almost at the end of his rope, Connelly encountered a quiet friendly banker named Rowland Stebbins, lured him to "109," and over a couple of Martinis persuaded him to be the play's angel. Crouse and Smith were approaching the door as Connelly emerged, wreathed in smiles, and introduced them to Stebbins: "Meet the sucker!" The opening of *The Green Pastures,* which won the Pulitzer Prize, was one of the triumphal moments in the American theater; and afterward we all hurried over to "109" to await Connelly with flowers and champagne and a child's blackboard on an easel inscribed: *Author! Author!* Marc arrived about midnight, carrying the early editions of the morning papers, and read aloud the rave reviews which pulled out all stops in their unanimous praise. "Silly fellows," he kept muttering in a strangely husky voice, "silly fellows."

On another evening at "109" a friend introduced me to a bespectacled and modest young advertising copywriter named Nash. He dabbled in light verse, he admitted over a drink, and after some urging he recited a sample. It has stuck in my mind all these years:

> The turtle lives 'twixt plated decks
> Which practically conceal its sex.
> I think it clever of the turtle
> In such a fix to be so fertile.

It was not until 1929 that Ogden Nash made his debut in *The New Yorker* with a verse which began: "Senator Smoot, Republican, Ut.,/Is planning a ban on Sex." His next contribution, called "Spring Comes to Murray Hill," employed for the first time the unique rhyme scheme (endlessly copied but never matched) which has earned him the uncontested title of Comic Poet Laureate of America: "I sit in an office at 244 Madison Avenue,/And say to myself, You have a responsible job, havenue?" Nash told me later, "In this one I first realized the possibilities of working from behind a mask of semi-literacy, and could say what I wanted to say without the self-consciousness which had previously paralyzed me." The British audience proved to be a little slow at catching on, he added; when a collection of his verse was reprinted in England, the London *Times Literary Supplement* commented: "Neat ideas, marred by careless rhyming."

They were mellow times, those speakeasy days, with good company and good talk, lighted with occasional shafts of pure wit. There was George Kaufman's celebrated sally when a pompous stranger bragged long and loud that his ancestry went back to the Crusades. Kaufman cocked his head, with the beady eye of a robin spotting an especially juicy worm. "I had an ancestor, Sir Roderick Kaufman, who also went on the Crusades," he said, and added after a brief pause, "as a spy." On another occasion Kaufman and Frank Sullivan and Edna Ferber were dining together on a dark and stormy night. Sleet rattled at the windows, and the conversation turned morbidly to suicide. Kaufman fingered his empty glass and confided that he was planning to kill himself. Miss Ferber was shocked. "How, George?" she gasped.

"With kindness," Kaufman replied resolutely, and signaled for another drink.

New York's private clubs had their own means of evading the Act. Most of them provided lockers where members could keep their bottles; but The Players, at 16 Gramercy Park, held stubbornly to its time-honored bar, and kept it open during the whole Prohibition era. Thanks to a little *pourboire* distributed here and there in the right places, the club was never raided; and laughter echoed uninterrupted over the click of pool balls and slap of playing cards in the historic downstairs grill, where Thomas Nast's original cartoon of the Tammany Tiger hangs on the wall and Mark Twain's pool cue is still in its place of honor above the rack.

Sixteen Gramercy Park was the home of Edwin Booth, who willed it to his friends in 1888 as a clubhouse for actors and artists and writers, a unique sanctum of the arts. The pleasantly dingy rooms with their patina of age, the architectural jumble of Italian marble and English wainscoting and blue Holland tiles, the Shakespearean mottoes over the fireplaces and furbelows on the ceilings, the oil portraits in rococo gilt frames that take up every inch of wall space lend the ancient building a sort of cluttered intimacy, as homey as an old-fashioned parlor. It is a club of great traditions, and the greatest, I think, is its tradition of good humor.

I was elected to its august fellowship at the unripe age of twenty-four; and on my first visit as a member I was halted by the frowning doorman, venerable John MacDonald. "Are you the new busboy?" he growled. "Use the service entrance." Being a callow freshman, I used to sit in silence while Irvin Cobb told his inimitable and (it seemed to me, even at my tender years) interminable Southern stories. Now and then Jack Barrymore and Booth Tarkington would home in on the club after a bibulous night on the town to recount their comic adventures. Sometimes I would see the great Don Marquis — silver mane and bushy black eyebrows and pallid tragic face — polishing his daily newspaper column at a corner table. Or Oliver Herford, squinting myopically through his monocle, resting an elbow on the bar while he cut an overblown member down to size.

Herford was The Players' great leveler. The painter Edward Simmons was cured of a tendency toward verbosity when Herford posted a warning sign over the door: EXIT IN CASE OF SIMMONS. It was the same Simmons who came to Herford in tears and complained that a fellow member had just offered him five hundred dollars to resign from the club. "Don't do it, old man," Herford advised him. "Hold out for a better offer."

One year, on the occasion of the Club's annual Ladies' Day (which Sullivan has described as "the nuptial flight of the queen bee") Herford volunteered to escort a visiting actress through The Players' upper recesses. In the hall outside the library they paused before a collection of plaster death masks, including the sunken and desiccated face of Richard Brinsley Sheridan. "Oh, he looks terrible," she shuddered. Herford explained mildly, "After all, my dear, he wasn't very well when it was taken."

I was standing at the bar with Herford the afternoon that a loud and aggressively masculine member strode down the stairs into the grill, wearing a shaggy orange-brown tweed jacket with a double row of leather buttons. He slapped Herford on the back, jolting the monocle out of his eye, and bellowed, "Well, Oliver, how d'ya like my new jacket?" Herford replaced the monocle. "I was just saying to my friend here as I saw you," he murmured, "who's the nursing Airedale bitch?"

If Herford was the rapier, F. P. Adams was the stiletto. Adams lived on Thirteenth Street, only a few blocks away, and spent much time in the grillroom playing pool, a pastime at which he did not like to be interrupted. Once he spotted a club bore (The Players had its quota) making for him across the room with hand outstretched, obviously about to speak. Adams grabbed his hand, said, "How are you that's fine," and returned to his game, leaving the member with hand still held out and mouth sagging.

Adams was an equally devout poker player, with a hard-core group which included Herbert ("Sheriff") Ransom, an actor whose expression when holding a pat hand was so revealing that F.P.A. suggested a club rule: "Anyone who looks at Ransom's face is cheating." It was at one of these sessions that Tom Chalmers mentioned the recent death of "Christy" Mathewson, the baseball pitcher, who had been a friend of a long-winded member and the subject of most of his wearisome anecdotes. "This will cut down his conversational stock fifty percent," Chalmers observed. "A drop in the bucket," Adams snapped.

A legendary club, and the legends are handed down over the years. Reginald Birch's ability to doze for twenty minutes while standing erect at the bar — an ability which prompted veteran actor John King to remark, "He's got cab-horse blood." F.P.A.'s good-natured jibe at Jack Shuttleworth, then editor of *Judge,* whose heart is as big as his stature is small: "If you were half a man — and you are." Rea Irvin, art editor of *The New Yorker,* executing a winning shot at pool and leading an impromptu parade around and around the table, followed by Sullivan and Norman Anthony and Paul Parks and Clive Weed and Rollin Kirby, all singing at the top of their lungs "The Stars and Stripes Forever." Don Marquis shouldering up to the bar, after a month on the wagon, and ordering a double Martini, with the proud announcement, "I've conquered my goddam will power."

Of all the members of The Players, back in those halcyon days, I stood most in awe of Don Marquis. Not that he was formidable — no one was ever more unaffected and modest — but I felt then (and I still do) that he had already become immortal in his time, that his poems of Archy the cockroach and

F.P.A. at the Players pool table, sketched from life by John Falter.
(Courtesy of the Players.)

Mehitabel the alley cat were an ageless American classic. I was not alone in my hero-worship; even the usually reserved F.P.A. wrote in "Diary of Our Own Mr. Pepys": "What a deeply humorous man Don is, and far closer to Mark Twain than anybody I know or am ever likely to know." And E. B. White (also immortal in his time) has called him "a very funny man, his product rich and satisfying, full of sad beauty, bawdy adventure, political wisdom, and wild surmise; full of pain and jollity, full of exact and inspired writing."

It was Marquis's wry conceit to pretend that the vers libre in his "Sun Dial" column was composed by a cockroach ("It would be one on me," he wrote a friend, "if I should be remembered longest for creating a cockroach character") who hámmered it out with his head on the office typewriter. In his first reference to Archy, he explained:

We came into our room earlier than usual in the morning, and discovered a gigantic cockroach jumping about upon the keys. He did not see us, and we watched him. He would climb painfully upon the framework of the machine and cast himself with all his force upon a key, head downward, and his weight and the impact of the blow were just sufficient to operate the machine, one slow letter after another. He could not work the capital letters, and he had a great deal of difficulty operating the mechanism that shifts the paper so that a fresh line may be started. We never saw a cockroach work so hard or perspire so freely in all our lives before. After about an hour of this frightfully difficult literary labor he fell to the floor exhausted, and we saw him creep feebly into a nest of the poems which are always there in profusion.

Congratulating ourselves that we had left a sheet of paper in the machine the night before so that all this work had not been in vain, we made an examination, and this is what we found:

expression is the need of my soul
i was once a vers libre bard

but i died and my soul went into the body of
   a cockroach
it has given me a new outlook upon life
i see things from the under side now
thank you for the apple peelings in your
   wastebasket
but your paste is getting so stale i cant eat it
there is a cat here called mehitabel i wish you
   would have
removed she nearly ate me the other night why dont she
catch rats that is what she is supposed to be for
there is a rat here she should get without delay

Archy protested in a subsequent nocturnal message that some of Marquis's readers were forever asking "how does archy work the shift so as to get a new line or how does archy do this or do that they are always interested in technical details when the main question is whether the stuff is literature or not." He had discovered that the soul of Mehitabel the cat formerly inhabited a human being ("at least that is what mehitabel is claiming these days") and quoted her dauntless song "Toujours Gai," here given in abbreviated version:

this is the song of mehitabel
of mehitabel the alley cat
as i wrote you before boss
mehitabel is a believer
in the pythagorean
theory of the transmigration
of the soul and she claims
that formerly her spirit
was incarnated in the body
of cleopatra
that was a long time ago
and one must not be
surprised if mehitabel

has forgotten some of her
regal manners

i have had my ups and downs
but wotthehell wotthehell
yesterday sceptres and crowns
fried oysters and velvet gowns
and today i herd with bums
but wotthehell wotthehell
i wake the world from sleep
as i caper and sing and leap
when i sing my wild free tune
wotthehell wotthehell
under the blear eyed moon
i am pelted with cast off shoon
but wotthchell wotthehell

    . . . . . . . .

i know that i am bound
for a journey down the sound
in the midst of a refuse mound
but wotthehell wotthehell
oh i should worry and fret
death and i will coquette
there s a dance in the old dame yet
toujours gai toujours gai

    . . . . . . . .

the things that i had not ought to
i do because i ve got to
wotthehell wotthehell
and i end with my favorite motto
toujours gai toujours gai

boss sometimes i think
that our friend mehitabel
is a trifle too gay

It was Don Marquis writing of himself, of course; for at heart he was a poet, and his life "followed the precarious pattern of a poet's existence," E. B. White said in his preface to *the lives and times of archy and mehitabel.* "He danced on bitter nights with Boreas, he ground out copy on drowsy afternoons when he felt no urge to write and in newspaper offices where he didn't want to be." His life was marked for tragedy. He earned a small fortune from his Broadway hit *The Old Soak* and lost it all on a religious play about the Crucifixion. In a short span of years, he suffered the death of a young son, then his first wife, then his daughter, and finally his second wife. Like Archy, after a lifetime of frightfully difficult literary labor, he fell exhausted. A series of strokes left him partly paralyzed and unable to work, and he was forced to tender his resignation from the club he loved because he could not afford to pay his dues. "My dear Dave," he wrote David McKinley, treasurer of The Players, "I have your letter in which you express the hope that Dame Fortune may be smiling on me. She is, but it is the most sarcastic goddam smile I ever saw on anyone's face. Yours sincerely, Don Marquis."

Frank Sullivan and a couple of fellow Players visited him at his sisters' home in Forest Hills a few weeks before his death. "Don was like the hero of a Greek tragedy," Sullivan wrote afterward, "one of those on whom the gods piled misfortune after misfortune until it seemed unbelievable. I never knew anyone who had such tragedy in his life as Don, and he wasn't even spared at the end. Poverty, a long dreadful sickness, paralysis, loss of faculties. . . . His doctor had told us at The Players to come in twos and threes because he couldn't talk and whoever visited him had to do most of the talking. When we left he cried, in great sobs . . . I can't bear to see anyone I like suffering, and to see anyone as great as Don in such a state of physical and mental wreckage was almost too much to bear."

Drawing by George Herriman for John Riddell (Corey Ford).

Some years before, when I was reviewing books for *Vanity Fair,* I suggested that his publishers bring out an illustrated edition of *archy and mehitabel* with drawings by George Herriman (another immortal) whose unconquerable *Krazy Kat,* half-feline and half-human, seemed to match the valiant soul of Mehitabel. Herriman's art, I felt, would be as ideally mated to Marquis's style as Gluyas Williams belonged with Robert Benchley. Doubleday, Doran and Company took up my proposal, to Marquis's delight, and Frank Crowninshield, editor of *Vanity Fair,* told me later that Don had described me in conversation as "a humorist with a sense of humor." It is the finest compliment I have ever received.

Though I did not know Marquis well, I had a letter from him once that I still cherish. I had published an article in *Vanity Fair* on the subject of Humor — sooner or later every young writer has to get an article on Humor off his chest — in which I listed my own selection of the greatest living humorists. The list began: "There's Don Marquis, of course . . ." That casual assumption of his preeminent position seemed to please Marquis, who never had any confidence in himself (again like Archy, the question was always whether the stuff was literature or not), and he sent me an emotional note of thanks from California, during one of his periods of forced labor in the cinema salt mines. He was miserable and bitter and hated Hollywood, he said, where "the flowers have no smell, the fruit has no taste, and the women have no milk in their breasts." I never heard from him again; but I have always been grateful that I wrote something which, at least for a moment, made him happy.

# 5

## *This Side of Parodies*

IN the first issue of *Vanity Fair,* which appeared shortly before the outbreak of World War I, Frank Crowninshield set down his editorial creed. He expressed unflagging confidence that "we, as a nation, have come to realize the need for more cheerfulness, for hiding a solemn face, for a fair measure of pluck, and for great good humor. *Vanity Fair* means to be as cheerful as anybody. It will print humor, it will look at the stage, at the arts, at the world of letters, at sport, and at the highly vitalized, electric, and diversified life of our day from the frankly cheerful angle of the optimist, or, which is much the same thing, from the mock-cheerful angle of the satirist."

*Vanity Fair* not only looked at the diversified life of the Twenties; it *was* the Twenties. Its approach was witty (but never gauche), sardonic (but never unmannerly, never rude), erudite (but, with perfect aplomb, never taking itself too seriously). It was more than the purveyor of smart table talk, a sort of Elbert Hubbard of the *soigné* upper crust. It created a high society of its own, sophisticated and artificial and snobbish, and it died in the impoverished Thirties when that society came to an end.

It was a handsome magazine, designed to lend prestige to the living-room table, profligate with gorgeous color reproductions of Picasso and Matisse and Van Gogh, with full-page photographs by Cecil Beaton and Bruehl and Genthe and the great Steichen, with a luminous list of celebrated contributors. It flattered its readers by assuming they were cultured — once it ran an article entirely in French — and offered them such avant-garde writers as Gertrude Stein (a poem entitled "Have They Attacked Mary. He Giggled") and D. H. Lawrence and T. S. Eliot. With the tacit admission that the best contemporary writing came from abroad, its pages were filled with imported names: Paul Morand, Ferenc Molnar, André Maurois, Lord Dunsany, P. G. Wodehouse, Colette, Cocteau, Somerset Maugham, and a then unknown young Englishman named Noel Coward. Among its American contributors were Nathan and Mencken, e. e. cummings, Alva Johnston, Broun, Sullivan, Dorothy Parker, Will Rogers, Edna St. Vincent Millay, who signed her stories Nancy Boyd, and in 1920 it ran the first published piece by a new hireling, Robert Benchley, with the uncharacteristic title: "No Matter from What Angle You Looked at It, Alice Brookhansen Was a Girl Whom You Would Hesitate to Invite into Your Own Home."

*Vanity Fair* prided itself on being a pioneer. It was the earliest magazine to recognize Negro artists, portrayed in Steichen's lovely camera studies of Paul Robeson and Florence Mills, the popular torch singer of *Bye, Bye, Blackbird,* or in his dramatic photograph of the March to the Promised Land in *The Green Pastures.* It introduced modern painters like Marie Laurencin and Raoul Dufy, causing its advertisers to protest about the "decadent and distorted" art in the magazine. There were cartoons by *Punch*'s George Belcher, wax figurines by Hidalgo (who described himself, with a straight face, as a half-

Aztec sculptor), and full-color caricatures by William Cotton
and Miguel Covarrubias.

Its pages, as you look back over them today, are a faithful
record of the era. Among the pictured or cartooned celebrities
of the theater and politics and sport (and so many of them have
already retreated into the shadows) were Nazimova, Tilly
Losch, Helen Hayes and Charles MacArthur, Lillian Gish, the
Barrymores, the Lunts, the Astaires, the Sitwells; Katherine
Cornell as Elizabeth Barrett Browning; Clarence Darrow,
photographed by Steichen at the time of the Leopold-Loeb trial:
George Bellows's canvas of Dempsey being knocked out of the
ring by Firpo; Henry Ford, Winston Churchill, Max Schmeling,
William T. Tilden, Amelia Earhart, and Aimee Semple Mc-
Pherson, who was nominated for Oblivion along with Chic
Sale, Raymond Duncan, Ursula (*Ex-Wife*) Parrott, Lou
Tellegen, Belle Livingston, Cornelius Vanderbilt, and Queen
Marie of Rumania.

The magazine was always capable of the unexpected. Weary
of its own monthly "Hall of Fame," it had founded the
irreverent "Hall of Oblivion." It featured a series of "Impossible Interviews" on which I collaborated with Covarrubias,
bringing together such ill-matched pairs as John D. Rockefeller,
Sr., vs. Josef Stalin, or Greta Garbo vs. Calvin Coolidge. Sometimes it invited a group of well-known personages to name the
Ten Dullest Authors (D. H. Lawrence won hands down), or to
Write Their Own Epitaphs (such as George S. Kaufman's
"Over my dead body!"; Dorothy Parker's "Excuse my dust!";
and Hirschfield's "Here lies the body of Harry Hirschfield —
if not, notify Ginsberg & Co., Undertakers, at once!"). Perhaps
it might ask erudite Joseph H. Choate to write about DeWolf
Hopper, or the cosmic Walter Lippmann to do an article on
"Peaches" and "Daddy" Browning. The incongruity, the in-
finite variety, the smartness that characterized *Vanity Fair* were

due largely to the fertile imagination of Frank Crowninshield.

He was an Edwardian gentleman, the mirror of graciousness, his body inclined in a half-bow, head forward and tilted slightly to one side, white hair brushed straight back from a furrowed forehead, mustache carefully waxed, one crescent-shaped pane of his pince-nez glasses held delicately between thumb and forefinger. The ghost of a smile usually haunted his lips, but they would pull back in a sharp grimace of pain when he was embarrassed or distressed. He was the soul of kindness, affectionate and considerate and thoughtful, his courtesy as flawless as his brocaded white waistcoat. "His manners were so perfect," a fellow editor observed, "that he seemed insincere." If an article of mine pleased him, he never failed to send me a letter, on his engraved blue stationery, expressing his gratitude in the most fulsome terms. Cleveland Amory, in his perceptive introduction to a recent *Vanity Fair* anthology, quotes a harassed writer: "Even his letters of rejection were so complimentary that they had to be read twice to discover whether he was making a nomination for the Pulitzer Prize or expressing regret." And Paul Gallico still recalls a note that accompanied a manuscript which Crowninshield returned to him. "My dear Paul," he wrote, "this is superb. A little masterpiece! What color! What life! How beautifully you have phrased it all! A veritable gem! — Why don't you take it around to *Harper's Bazaar?*"

I've known a half-dozen great editors in my lifetime, but none of them had Crownie's peculiar flair. He was a polished after-dinner speaker, a *bon vivant* and authority on good wines (though he never drank), and a man of keen wit — "Married men," he remarked once, "make very poor husbands." He also possessed a native shrewdness, inherited from his New Bedford whaling ancestors, and was not above buying up the canvases of an unknown artist, publicizing his work in *Vanity Fair* until it became a vogue, and then selling the originals he had acquired at a handsome profit. Now and then he showed a trace of Yankee prudishness. I had written an article about the Canadian Rockies, in which I described the train "worming its way on its black belly across spidery trestles." Crownie called me into his office in an agony of embarrassment. "Dear boy," he began (he always addressed me as "dear boy" or by my first name, which he pronounced "cow-rih"), "we really can't use the word 'belly' in *Vanity Fair.*"

Robert Benchley had a similar experience when he wrote an article for Crowninshield on "The Social Life of the Newt," which contained a thoroughly innocuous account of its mating habits, based on his own conception of newt sexual relations, which was less than nil. His account disturbed Crownie's sensitivities, and he asked Benchley to rewrite it so that it would not offend the *Vanity Fair* readers. The resulting chaste description of a newt's courtship — in which the male's power of observation was tested by substituting another (but less charming) female, a bronze paperweight shaped like a newt, and finally a common rubber eraser — was one of Benchley's most successful pieces.

Crowninshield had an uncanny instinct for discovering new talent. Thomas Wolfe's first story, "The Bums at Sunset," appeared in his magazine. In 1920 he hired young Bob Sherwood, just home after valiant war service, and a little lady with dark bangs named Dorothy Rothschild, whose initial printed effort (and not a very accurate forecast of the later work which she would sign Dorothy Parker) was a caption under a display of women's underwear: "Brevity is the soul of lingerie, as the Petticoat said to the Chemise." Nothing in his entire career distressed him more, he confided to me, than Condé Nast's order to fire Mrs. Parker. But he was helpless; Nast was the owner.

Condé Nast approached him in 1914, when Crowninshield was art editor of the *Century*. (He had been publisher of *The Bookman* before 1900, and later edited *Metropolitan* and *Munsey's*.) Nast was planning a new magazine, to be called *Dress & Vanity Fair*, and he asked Crownie to be its editor. With infallible instinct, his first act was to eliminate *Dress &* from the title. He refused for a long time to include a department on "The Well-Dressed Man," explaining suavely, "A gentleman *knows* how to dress."

The *Vanity Fair* offices were located on the nineteenth floor of the Graybar Building on Lexington Avenue, adjoining Grand Central Terminal; and they reflected Crownie's ebullient good spirits. Jeanne Ballot was his devoted secretary, tagging after him with stenographer's pad poised as he dictated his letters on the run. His managing editor was Don Freeman, an overburdened young man who trudged up and down the corridors all day with an armload of galley proofs and a brow wrinkled with care. On his staff, during the Twenties, were novelist Richard Sherman; Finley Peter Dunne, Jr.; David Cort, who had followed me as editor of *Jester* and whose brilliant mind contributed immeasurably to the John Riddell parody series; Lois Long; and Margaret Case Harriman, talented daughter of the proprietor of the Algonquin and *Vanity Fair*'s liaison with the Round Table. When word got out in 1924 that Harold Ross was planning a new magazine to be called *The New Yorker*, Lois Long quit *Vanity Fair* to work for Ross, but Maggie Harriman was reluctant to give up her guaranteed forty dollars a week for an uncertain venture. On the day that the first issue of *The New Yorker* appeared, Maggie recalled in *The Vicious Circle*, Crownie summoned her to his private sanctum, and went through the rival publication page by page, nibbling square mints and pondering. At last he leaned back in his chair in relief and removed his pince-nez. "Well, Margaret," he said cheerfully, "I think we have nothing to fear." Ten years later *The New Yorker* was to drive his magazine out of business.

Cheerfulness was the word for the *Vanity Fair* offices, though the startled Mr. Nast, peering incredulously through the door, might have preferred the word lunacy. There were the Keene Twins, a pair of dancing sisters who had temporarily deserted musical comedy to work as file clerks. They kept themselves in shape for their profession by doing limbering and stretching exercises besides the water cooler, or pulling out all the top drawers of the files and dancing past the cabinets, kicking the drawers back in place one by one. Sometimes Crownie, an amateur magician, would call the staff together to demonstrate a new card trick, or vie with his friend John Mulholland at feats of legerdemain involving canaries or coins. Again, all production would be halted while the editor organized an office game of charades, and on payday it was his invariable custom to adjourn business and take the office girls to lunch at Schrafft's.

Another prominent staff member, and later managing editor, was Clare Boothe or Clare Boothe Brokaw or Clare Boothe Luce (my chronology gets a little muddy). Her classic beauty was widely admired, her books were acclaimed as masterpieces by the critics of *Life* and *Time,* and her reputation for wit was held high until she had the ill-fortune to tangle with Mrs. Parker. As they were leaving "21" one evening, they collided in the doorway. Clare stepped back and gestured Mrs. Parker to precede her with an edged smile: "Age before beauty." "Pearls before swine," Mrs. Parker replied, and strode through the door.

I was reminded of Clare not long ago when I was in need of a copy of one of my collections of *Vanity Fair* parodies. I called my favorite secondhand bookstore, run by the O'Malley Brothers on lower Park Avenue. Yes, they had a complete set of the John Riddell books, recently purchased from the owner. I hurried over and found the set intact, each book affectionately inscribed "To Clare from Corey."

I still have my autographed copy of Clare's *Stuffed Shirts,* in case O'Malley's is interested.

The genesis of the John Riddell parodies was typical of Crownie. One morning, out of a clear sky, he phoned and invited me to lunch. I assumed it would be at the Knickerbocker Club or the Coffee House; but Crownie, always unpredictable, escorted me downstairs to the Oyster Bar in Grand Central. There we sat on adjoining stools and sipped our oyster stew while Crownie raised his voice to be heard above the clamor of the crowded bar: "I have an idea, Cowrih. Would you pass the crackers, thank you. Why don't you do a monthly book review for us? Pepper, please. Perhaps in the form of a parody of a current best seller. So sorry to trouble you, waiter, may we have some more coffee? Think it over, dear boy. Dessert?" Thus the casual beginning of a series which ran each month for almost ten years, and was collected in three successive anthologies.

Since I was already writing a monthly article for *Vanity Fair,* I decided to sign the parodies with a nom de plume. My method of selecting a pseudonym (unfortunately I did not have Mr. Stratemeyer's mother to help me out) was to shut my eyes, open the New York Telephone Directory at random, and put my finger on a name. The name turned out to be Runkleschmelz, so I threw the phone book away and thought up "John Riddell," a clever rearrangement of the letters of my own name.

It was my great good fortune to have Miguel Covarrubias assigned to the Riddell series as illustrator. Miguel was one of America's most penetrating and ruthless caricaturists, a quiet little Mexican with the dimpled face of a cherub and innocent brown eyes that were as misleading as Mrs. Parker's demure smile. Miguel carried a concealed dirk in his sleeve, which he

Corey Ford as John Riddell by Covarrubias.

Will Rogers by Covarrubias. From *The John Riddell Murder Case.*

used with deadly effect in his cartoon of Will Rogers as a Drug-
store Cowboy with an unwinding lariat for a mouth, or of
Sinclair Lewis, sporting sleeve garters and an enormous Elk's
charm on his watch chain, as Mr. Babbitt himself. Rogers loved
his caricature, but Lewis never forgave *Vanity Fair.*

One of my early parodies was of Katherine Brush's best-
selling *Young Man of Manhattan,* and Covarrubias, who preferred to work from live subjects rather than photographs,
asked to meet her. Kay Brush had used her sizable royalties to
purchase a vast triplex apartment over by the East River. A
butler ushered us into the echoing foyer, decorated with shields
and suits of armor and Persian rugs draped from the railing of
the second-floor balcony. As we waited below, slightly overwhelmed, Kay made a dramatic entrance, floating down the
marble staircase in a red satin gown and greeting Covarrubias in
her best hostess manner. "And how do you like my little apartment?" she asked, waving a modest hand at the baronial hall.
Miguel dimpled. "What a place to show Packards," he said
pleasantly.

I had planned to keep the identity of "John Riddell" secret,
but it was revealed through an unhappy incident. I had selected
for my next subject a Southern lady novelist named Frances
Newman, who had just published an atrocious story of unrequited passion entitled *Dead Lovers Are Faithful Lovers.* In
my parody, called "Dead Novelists Are Good Novelists," I
described her heroine leaping out of a window because her
novel was not loved by John Riddell. It began in Miss Newman's redundant style:

When the little male cuckoo that was only a wooden cuckoo
hopped out of a tiny mahogany door to cry his name three times in
six beautifully separate syllables, Isabel Evelyn slipped off the long
black-clocked sheer silk stocking from her beautifully tended right

foot. And when she slipped off the long black-clocked sheer silk stocking from her beautifully tended left foot, the little wooden cuckoo did not hop out of his tiny mahogany door to cry his name in two more beautifully separate syllables, because it was only three o'clock and a fourth "Cuck-oo" right then would have sounded silly. But when she stood up and slipped off from her beautifully rounded shoulders the beautifully embroidered white chemise which her mother had bought her for $2.98 in Gimbel's basement, the little male cuckoo *did* open the tiny mahogany door and hop out again just for a moment, on the pretext that he had forgotten his rubbers, because he was only a wooden cuckoo but he had the instincts.

When she had laid the beautifully embroidered white chemise across the bottom of a bed that was a bookcase in the daytime, she walked across the yellow hooked rug that her great-grandmother had hooked from a furniture store in Fall River in 1843, and she looked into the full length mirror, which had been presented to her by a wealthy Chicago packer because it was the precise reflection of her beautifully tended figure, at the familiar arrangement of hair and eyes and nose and lips which could be called a face if you were being generous enough. And when she looked down at the delicately curved throat and the voluptuous arms and the two round firm white objects which reminded her of two round firm white pint-bottles of cream which the Borden's man left on her doorstep every morning, but which were really only her two fists clenched tightly before her, a heavy golden shell of pain burst in the center of her body for fear that John Riddell did not love her . . .

The issue of *Vanity Fair* which contained the parody was on the stands, and my first Riddell collection in which it was included had already gone to press, when the headlines announced that Miss Newman had committed suicide, not by leaping out of the window but by taking an overdose of sleeping pills. To make matters worse, the story reported that a copy of *Vanity Fair* was found in her room, opened to my parody with its prophetic title. I was widely denounced, by my

real name, as an unmitigated rogue, chivalrous Southern newspapers warned me never to set foot below the Mason-Dixon
line, suh, and my publishers debated whether to scrap the Riddell book entirely. It appeared at last, with an insert explaining
the unfortunate circumstances of Miss Newman's demise; but
from then on, whenever I parodied anyone, I took a morbid
interest in the obituary columns until the article was safely in
print.

Ernest Hemingway offered an irresistible temptation to a
parodist, of course. It was my opinion at the time (and I still
think the criticism is valid) that Hemingway was a superb short
story writer — "The Snows of Kilimanjaro" is an enduring
classic — but in his longer works he tended to sink his point too
deep and the novel foundered. I tried to bring this out in a
lampoon of his bull-fighting stories called "Corto y Derecho":

"How are you going yourself, Ernest?" I asked him.
"You seen this *Men Without Women?*" he says.
"I seen it everywheres."
"Well," says Ernest, "I'm going to need a lot of luck with that
book."
"They can't beat you, Ernest," said the waiter, "they can't beat you
in the short fights."
"Sure," I said. "There's nobody can handle his dialogue like you
do. You'll beat them all."
"Maybe," says Ernest. "Sure. I got a chance."
"Handle them like you handled *The Snows of Kilimanjaro.*"
"Or *Fifty Grand,*" said the coffee-boy.
"*Corto y derecho,*" he says. "Short and straight."

I was sitting at a table at the edge of the arena, sipping *Anis del
Toro,* and Hemingway was in the center of the ring, under the lights,
fighting a bull. As he flung open his dialogue with both hands, the
bull charged, tail up. Hemingway swung his plot clear and, as the
bull recharged, brought around his dialogue in a half-circle that
pulled the bull to his knees. We all applauded.

"Why, he's a great bull-fighter," the coffee-boy said.

"They're all trying to imitate him," I said.

"He's all right," said the waiter, resting his bottle on his hip. "He's all right so long as he doesn't drive his point too deep."

"Sure," I said, "maybe he won't last very long in the big fights. But right now he's got everything."

"Huh," said Hemingway, *"toro!"* The bull was standing, his four feet square, his head low. Hemingway furled his dialogue with his left hand. The bull's eyes watched him. We all leaned forward.

"He's the greatest fighter in America," the coffee-boy said.

"He's the greatest fighter in America," said the waiter, ."in the short fights."

"Watch this," Ernest says, "this is going to be good."

As he spoke, Hemingway drew forth the point of his story from the folds of his dialogue, profiled it on the horns of the bull and, rising on his toes, sighted along the plot toward the climax high up on the bull's shoulders.

"Keep up that dialogue," I said, "and nothing can touch you."

"Do I look as if I'd last?"

"Sure you'll last," says the coffee-boy. "You could run ten editions the way you look right now."

*Corto y derecho* Hemingway lanced himself on the bull. There was a shock, and then he felt himself go up in the air. He pushed on the point as he went up and over, and it flew out of his hand, end-over-ending out of the story.

"Look out, Ernest," I says.

He lit on the ground, and the bull was on him. Hemingway, lying on the ground, kicked with his slippered feet like a man keeping a ball in the air. The bull lowered his head.

"What do you say, Ernest?" asked the bull.

"I'm going good," said Hemingway, "I'm going great."

"Sure," said the bull. "You're upside down, that's all."

"What happened?" he asked.

"You tried to drive your point home," said the bull, "and I threw you."

"Let's have a drink," he says, rising to his feet.

"Don't you want to fight any more today?" said the bull.

"No, I'd rather sit and talk," said Ernest. "I'd rather talk than fight any day."

They walked across the ring, and the bull pulled several banderillas out of his shoulder and straightened his horns. They came over to my table.

"I want you to meet my friend, Mr. Riddell," said Hemingway. "John, this is the bull."

"Well," said the bull.

"Three *Anis del Toro*," I said to the waiter.

"These drinks are on me, by the way," the bull said.

"No, I've got it," says Ernest.

"I'll toss you for it," said the bull, lowering his horns.

The waiter paused with the bottle on his hip. "Do you want them with water, Ernest?" he said.

"No, I'll take mine straight," says Ernest. "Short and straight."

*"Corto y derecho,"* said the waiter.

"That's right," Ernest says.

The waiter filled the glasses.

Some years later, in Hollywood, Scott Fitzgerald told me a revealing sequel. Hemingway, who was something of a sadist, had been badgering his friend unmercifully, in person and in print — in his first version of "The Snows of Kilimanjaro" he had gone so far as to mention Scott by name and describe his addiction to drink, his weakness, his failure as an artist — and Scott was deeply hurt. They were seated together at the Ritz Bar in Paris, Scott said, on the day that my *Vanity Fair* parody appeared. Scott insisted on reading it aloud, and when Hemingway showed increasing irritation he read it a second time. Evidently the point had driven home, for Hemingway strode out of the Ritz in a huff. *Corto y derecho.*

I was never close to H. L. Mencken or George Jean Nathan. Our potential friendship withered when I submitted an article to their jointly edited magazine, *The Smart Set,* and it was returned the same day with a special delivery stamp. This seemed to me a little gratuitous; but I enjoyed Mencken's boldness, even his affected Katzenjammer style, and I marveled at Nathan's sustained sneer. Their partnership ended when Mencken elbowed Nathan out and assumed sole editorship of the new *American Mercury.* I made use of this incident in a parody called "The Bridge of San Thornton Wilder," after the current best seller. Mencken was amused by my parody, Crownie reported afterward, but Nathan refused to write for *Vanity Fair* again, a blow which the magazine managed to survive:

One day twin boys were discovered in the foundlings' basket before the door of the Convent of Santa Borzoi Alfred Samuel de las Blanches. Names were applied to them almost before the arrival of the wet-nurse, and indeed names have been applied to them with considerable vigor ever since. As they grew up they gradually assumed the profession of the scribe, and made a fair living condemning plays, denouncing books, and publishing a monthly magazine called *The Smart Set,* wherein they achieved a reputation of sorts by refusing to approve of anything.

From the years when they first learned to speak, they invented a language for themselves, one that no one else could understand. This language was a curious mixture of old Teutonic phrases and 1890 slang words, such as *sitzplatz* and *flapdoodle,* and it was the symbol of their profound identity with one another. No word is adequate to describe the mutual admiration of these brothers. There existed a oneness so terrible that they could not recognize anyone else as their intellectual equal.

But at last a shadow fell across this unity. One night there was a light tap at their bedroom door, and the brother named Manuel opened to admit a visitor in a conspicuous jade-colored jacket. She said hurriedly: "You are H. L. Manuel, yes? You write about letters, do you not? I want you to write about letters for me, please."

"Yes, señora. You can trust me to do anything for you."

"Do you swear by everything holy?"

"There is nothing holy to me, señora. I will do my best."

"Here is your reward." She showed him his name, printed in very large letters: "H. L. Manuel, Editor of the *American Mercury*," and then folding her green jacket about her she left the room. Manuel put his hands over his ears, rested his elbows on his knees, and stared at his name fascinated. He became aware that his brother Estaban was preparing to leave.

"Come back, you *dummkopf.*" He was talking in their secret language. *"Was ist los mit dir,* Estaban?"

George Jean Estaban stood in the dark of the open door. In the unnatural voice in which we make the greatest declarations of our lives, he muttered, "I'm in your way." Carrying his own ideas packed in a very small bag, Estaban set out by himself on the road to Posterity; and it was in this manner that he approached the Bridge of San Thornton Wilder.

Of course, that is the trouble with this kind of plot. As soon as I said that he was approaching the Bridge of San Thornton Wilder, you knew perfectly well what was going to happen.

And, sure enough, it happened.

An unexpected by-product of the John Riddell series, and one which I look back on with relish, was an encounter with Theodore Dreiser. I had taken on the distinguished author of *An American Tragedy* in a parody called "Blueprints for Another American Tragedy" in which Mr. Dreiser, as president of the American Fiction Hauling and Construction Company, was utilizing the quarter-million words of his earlier novel to build an even more ponderous tome which, like the Roman viaducts or the Chinese Wall, had an excellent chance of lasting forever, if only because no one would ever have the patience to tear it down again. It opened in Dreiser's laborious prose, with his characteristic lapses in grammar and curiously dated dialogue:

Theodore Dreiser by Covarrubias. From *Meaning No Offense*.

Dusk — of a summer night.

And the tall walls of an American novel of perhaps 250,000 words — such walls as in time may linger as a mere fable.

And in the center of this tall edifice, or building, a solitary man working alone very patiently by himself — a man of about fifty years, with blue overalls, heavily built, yet not stout, perhaps five feet ten inches or five feet eleven inches in height, wearing a khaki shirt, with grey hair, white socks, a slight stoop, also suspenders, holding in one hand a hod, similar to the hod which is carried by a hod-carrier in one hand, and in the other hand a small trowel, or spade, like the spade, or trowel, carried by another hod-carrier, or else by the same hod-carrier in the other hand, provided there is nothing in the other hand of this first hod-carrier at the time, such as a carnation.

This tall, heavily built, yet not stout, man works, or *worked,* because our description is over now, very patiently, sweating in silence, like an elephant piling one block on top of another block with his trunk, except that this man who we are speaking of had no trunk, although on the other hand he wore, unlike an elephant, blue overalls. He would pick up the first block, or the second block, and place it on top of the third, or first, block, adding to that the second, or third, or first, block, depending on the order in which he had picked them up. Before he placed each block on top of the next block, however, he would first pat the top of the preceding block with his trowel, or spade, in order to cover it with cement, a process which, however, was not very successful, owing to the fact that he had no cement on his spade, or trowel, and therefore all three blocks would fall to the ground again where they had been before, and he would burst into tears.

At this John Riddell — myself, as I chanced to be — who, up to this point, had taken no part in the conversation, there being no conversation to take part in, said:

"What are these blocks which you are removing, or rearranging, by endeavoring to pile them up again?"

At this the man in blue overalls, slightly stooped over, arose to his feet, addressing the other man who had asked him the preceding question.

"Dese blocks dat youse see," he began, speaking in the up-to-date colloquialisms which he so often employed to indicate an uncouth laborer, "are paragraphs from *An American Tragedy* which I am presently dismantling, in order ter construct a bigger novel, Hully gee. Upsedaisy."

"But how can you make the paragraphs fit together again?" this from another passer-by, a stranger.

"I may not have much idea of what youse call construction," replied the speaker in blue overalls, the man who was being addressed by the other, "but I got lots of patience. I got all de patience in de woild. All de time in de woild. All de woids in de woild."

The younger, and shorter, of the two men, John Riddell, looked at the blueprints in the hand of the other man, who was older than he, likewise his senior.

"How many stories will there be?" he inquired.

"Just one story," the other replied. "De same story I always use. Boy loves girl, bip! — tragedy. Dat's life. Hot dam. *Git* a horse!"

A couple of days after my parody was published, the phone rang in the apartment on Beekman Place which I was sharing with Frank Sullivan, and an unfamiliar voice said, "This is Theodore Dreiser." Assuming that one of my fun-loving friends was having me on, I replied, "Why, hello, there, Ted." The voice continued: "I wanted to tell you how much I enjoyed your parody. I'd like to buy you a drink."

"Say, that would be peachy, hully gee, upsedaisy," I parried.

"I'm at a little bar on First Avenue." He gave the address. "Could you come over and join me?"

"Sure, I'll be there before you can say 23 skiddoo," I laughed, and my caller hung up.

I replaced the phone in its cradle, and sat staring at it for a moment. Suppose it wasn't a gag, I reflected uneasily. Suppose — just suppose — it was really Theodore Dreiser. Another and more disturbing thought occurred to me. Maybe he was angry about the parody, and was trying to lure me into his clutches. Maybe he had a couple of goons on hand to beat me up. I crossed the apartment to Sullivan's room, and laid the whole matter before him, and asked his advice.

"I think you ought to go over and see," he said. "After all, he invited you."

"Don't you want to come along with me, just for moral support?"

Sullivan, never one to let down a friend, replied loyally, "Certainly not, Ford. You got yourself into this. It's your problem."

I walked over to First Avenue very slowly, and tried to peer through the window of the place as I passed, but the shades were drawn. I continued to the corner, turned, and strolled back down the Avenue. Well, I might as well get it over with, I told myself. If I wind up in a slab of concrete at the bottom of the East River, Sullivan will be sorry. I opened the door, and blinked at the darkness. The place was empty, save for a lone figure at the bar, who waved to me. "John Riddell? I'm Dreiser. What will you have?"

I don't know how long we sat there, sipping and talking, but I know I've never met a nicer person or had a more drunken afternoon. It was dark when I wove my way back to the apartment. Sullivan peered at me curiously: "How did it go?"

"Peachy, you coward," I said. "Hot dam. *Git* a horse!" And I collapsed on the living-room sofa.

# 6

## My Ugly Roomer

ONCE American comedy gets its feet off the ground, it has no equal anywhere. The topsy-turvy exaggeration, the art of giddy idiocy which reached its height during the Twenties, is our native humor at its best; and Frank Sullivan is its acknowledged master. His association of ideas is lightning fast. He plods along a banal sentence, lips pursed in mock seriousness, until he stumbles on a word or phrase which people have been mouthing emptily all these years. Abruptly he takes off from it at a tangent no one ever thought of before, and zooms into a rarefied ether where mice talk, time turns back, zithers play, and a whole lunatic Lewis Carroll world lies upside down before him.

Let us say he is investigating a subject in the Encyclopedia, and the reference tells him to look under Louis XIV. So he looks under Louis XIV. "What are you looking under me for?" Louis XIV asks indignantly; and the rest of the column is a wildly illogical dialogue between Louis and Sullivan.

Or the snow is swirling down in bitter, icy swirls (he writes in "The Temptation of Anthony") but S. L. Rothafel nevertheless has ordered a faithless Roxy Theater usher thrown out into the storm. "You wouldn't put a dog out on a night like this," Sullivan protests. "Oh, wouldn't I?" says Roxy, and seizing a dog he puts him out.

Or Beatrice Lillie, in private life Lady Peel, has led him into the waiting room of the Pennsylvania Terminal, which she has taken furnished for the season, to chip him off a piece of the Peel emerald. "Have you a hammer on you?" she asks. "I always carry a hammer," Sullivan replies. "You never can tell when you may come upon a nail."

Or a young reader named Herbert Lester writes a postcard to the *World:* "I would like to have some information on Frank Sullivan, your columnist." Sullivan replies to Herbert:

Well, sonny, you are not the only one who would like to get some outside information on this bird. We would too, and we promise to cooperate with you if you promise to let us in on anything you happen to hear about him.

We don't know who he is, and we have moments when, not giving you any short answer, we think he isn't. Yesterday a little man with a long white beard and a Western Union uniform came in, sat down at a typewriter, and wrote a long piece which he handed to us.

"What's this?" we asked.

"Why, it's my copy," he said. "I'm Frank Sullivan."

Our gorge rose.

"No sense letting your gorge get the best of you," said the little man. "You can't solve this sullivan problem that way. The sooner you realize that sullivan is an abstract entity, the better off you'll be. Sullivan is the rain, and the frost on the pumpkin, and the twinkling stars at night, and the bloom on a pretty maid's cheek. It's the glance of an honest man at the woman he loves. It's the dew on the cobweb in the morning, and the opalescence of a bubble in a glass of ruby wine, and the lullaby of a mother to her babe. It's everything that is tender and lovely and beautiful and good. That's sullivan."

No quality such as Sullivan's can be caught in random quotations. It is too swift, too elusive; the sparks fly unexpectedly from the hammered steel and they cannot be preserved, they are gone instantly. He is inordinately tickled by the incongruous: cassowaries, cornets, Queen Mary's umbrella, kettledrummers, the gambusia, potato bugs, the fallacy of biting raw cops, and whether admirals should shave. Sometimes the laughter lies in a bizarre juxtaposition, like the overbearing attitude of Victor the Cat or the suicidal complex of Pierrot the Lovelorn Fly; sometimes it is provoked by an unusual name, as when a lady motorist is inviting a courteous traffic policeman to tea: "Shall we say — Puget Sound?" "Puget Sound would be fine, Mrs. Whettum"; sometimes it depends on his ear for trite phrases — "You are a cad and a fellow" or "I'll be bound" — and shopworn clichés of everyday speech. One of the most successful series in *The New Yorker* was his "The Cliché Expert Takes the Stand," in which Mr. Arbuthnot is grilled on such varied subjects as Politics, the Weather, Roosevelt-Hating, the Movies, or Love:

Q.  Mr. Arbuthnot, as an expert in the use of the cliché, are you prepared to testify here today regarding its application in topics of love, sex, matrimony and the like?
A.  I am.
Q.  Very good. Now, Mr. Arbuthnot, what's love?
A.  Love is blind.
Q.  Good. What does love do?
A.  Love makes the world go round.
Q.  Whom does a young man fall in love with?
A.  With the Only Girl in the World.
Q.  Whom does a young woman fall in love with?
A.  With the Only Boy in the World.
Q.  They are then said to be?
A.  Victims of Cupid's darts.
Q.  And he?
A.  Whispers sweet nothings in her ear.
Q.  Describe the Only Girl in the World.

A. Her eyes are like stars. Her teeth are like pearls. Her lips are ruby. Her cheek is damask, and her form divine.

Q. Haven't you forgotten something?

A. Eyes, teeth, lips, cheek, form — no, sir, I don't think so.

Q. Her hair?

A. Oh, certainly. How stupid of me. She has hair like spun gold.

Q. Very good, Mr. Arbuthnot. Now will you describe the Only Man?

A. He is a blond Viking, a he-man, and a square shooter who plays the game. There is something about him that rings true, and he has kept himself pure and clean so that when he meets the girl of his choice, the future mother of his children, he can look her in the eye.

Q. How?

A. Without flinching.

Q. Now, Mr. Arbuthnot, when the Only Man falls in love, madly, with the Only Girl, what does he do?

A. He walks on air.

Q. Yes, I know, but what is it he pops?

A. Oh, excuse me. The question, of course.

Q. Then what do they plight?

A. Their troth.

Q. Mr. Arbuthnot, your explanation of the correct application of the cliché in these matters has been most instructive, and I know that all of us cliché-users here will know exactly how to respond hereafter when, during a conversation, sex — when sex — ah —

A. I think what you want to say is "When sex rears its ugly head," isn't it?

Q. Thank you, Mr. Arbuthnot. Thank you very much.

A. Thank *you.*


Today Sullivan is the dean of living American humorists; his essays have been collected in half a dozen books (the title of one, *Broccoli and Old Lace,* was adapted by Lindsay and Crouse for their Broadway hit) and reprinted in countless anthologies; but never, for my taste, has he surpassed the dizzy heights of his "Interview with Lillian Gish," written for the Sunday drama page of the *World*. Mr. Sullivan, it develops, has forced his way past the Gish butler by the ingenious device of tossing a wig of golden curls about his head and posing as Mary Pickford. He and Miss Gish embrace, and then she holds him at arm's length, and studies him more closely. "But you're not Mary Pickford," she says after a moment of deliberation.

"I'm sorry," Sullivan explains glibly. "I'm the President of the United States."

Miss Gish sneers. "Oh, you are, are you? Very well, then, perhaps you can explain who this gentleman is!" and she opens a curtain, and there in the conservatory stands President Coolidge.

"I made a mistake," apologizes Sullivan. "I'm not the President, of course. I'm really the Vice-President."

"Is that so!" says the butler, and snatching off his side-whiskers he stands revealed as Vice-President Dawes.

Things are coming too fast for Sullivan. He decides to make a clean breast of it.

"My intentions were honest," he tells them. "I was only trying to draw Miss Gish into an interview. I won't lie to you any more. I'm Frank Sullivan."

They all start laughing, and President Coolidge says, "Is that so!" and opens a door, and there stands Frank Sullivan. . . .

Despite the bold ruses that he ascribes to himself in print, Sullivan personally is so modest and unassuming that Woollcott once called him "that timorous little omadhaun." He was born in Saratoga Springs, within a horseshoe's throw of the race track, and progressed to Cornell, then to a second lieutenancy in World War I, and finally to New York in 1919 as a reporter on the *Herald*. "I hope a young man starting in New York today has as good a time as I had," he says. He moved to the *Sun* the following year, and when Don Marquis quit he took over "The Sun Dial." In 1922 he joined the *World* staff and subbed for both F.P.A. and Broun in their columns on the famous op-ed feature page. He kept his old desk in the city room, and stubbornly resisted a by-line of his own until Herbert Bayard Swope, the *World*'s dynamic editor, insisted on a signed column in 1925. "Out of a Clear Sky" ran three times a week without interruption until the end of the *World* in 1931.

Since Sullivan and I were both bachelors and living alone — both my parents had died within six months — I suggested late in the Twenties that we might share an apartment together. Sullivan was agreeable (at least, he was agreeable to the suggestion) and we took a twelfth-floor flat at 433 East 51st Street, with a fine view of Beekman Place and, if you craned your neck far enough, the East River. We named the apartment: "Cloister on the Half Shell," and Sullivan dubbed himself "Ford's Ugly Roomer."

They were comfortable diggings: two bedrooms, a combination kitchen and dining alcove, and a beamed Tudor-style living room with brick fireplace and oak-paneled walls, decorated with a Dyak war shield and blowpipes and poisoned arrows which I had brought back after spending several months with the headhunters of central Dutch Borneo. (Consider that said very casually.) The display so intrigued Marc Connelly on his first visit that he grabbed a poker, pointed to the shield and spears, and embarked on a half-hour illustrated travelogue in the manner of Martin and Osa Johnson: "And so, armed with these crude native weapons, our little *safari* left Kookamonga on rhinoceros-back, bound for the burning *veldt* in quest of a zebra we could photograph with Osa because it matched her striped black-and-white serge suit. . . ."

Our housekeeper was Mrs. Annie Moffett, an apple-cheeked Scottish lady who bore such a striking resemblance to Queen Victoria that Sullivan refused to let her serve him in his room on a tray. "I can't have Queen Victoria bringing me breakfast in bed," he said nervously. She was an excellent cook, and on one of the rare occasions that we dined together Sullivan took a large second helping which he was unable to finish. "My eyes were bigger than my stomach," he apologized to Annie, and then looked down ruefully at his lap and added, "but my stomach's catching up with them fast."

It was a sort of Box and Cox arrangement. I worked all day while Sullivan slept, and he prowled all night while I was in bed. Virtually the only time we met was at Jim Moriarty's "109," after which I would go home while my Ugly Roomer continued on his appointed rounds to Dan's, then Tony's, then Bleeck's, then a final nightcap at Lou Richman's "Dizzy Club," patronized by a favorite hanger-on who described himself dolefully as "The Last Rose of the Mohicans." Sullivan was seated at the Dizzy Club bar one dawn when three strangers on adjoining stools got into a discussion of a World Series game. Sull, slightly foxed with alcohol, broke in and berated them roundly for a mistake they had made. Lou Richman interrupted the argument and lured him away to a side table, and plied him with coffee until the strangers departed. Then Sullivan learned that his adversaries were the gangster "Legs" Diamond and two of his hatchet men, who usually settled arguments by placing their opponent in a barrel of cement and dumping him in the bay.

Wending his way back to our apartment after another bibulous night on the town, Sullivan took to brooding about Supreme Court Justice McReynolds, who was reported to have called Franklin D. Roosevelt "that crippled s.o.b. in the White House." Burning with righteous indignation, Sullivan dashed off a blistering letter to Justice McReynolds, sealed the envelope with a satisfied pound of his fist, and dropped it down the mail chute by the elevator. It was not until he had undressed and climbed into bed that doubts assailed him about what he had done. After all, you don't go around insulting Supreme Court Justices by mail. Probably the F.B.I. would be on his track in the morning. In a panic of remorse, Sullivan dressed again, hurried down to the lobby and paced the floor for several hours till a postman arrived who unlocked the mailbox and allowed him to retrieve his letter and burn it.

Sullivan has a deep aversion to being made conspicuous in public, and he still cringes at the memory of an encounter with Mrs. Kathleen Norris, whose romantic novels betrayed no sign of her rich Irish sense of humor. Spotting the famed novelist looking into a shop window on Fifth Avenue, Sullivan came up behind her and playfully asked her for a dime for a cup of coffee. Mrs. Norris whirled on him, showing no sign of recognition, and raised her voice in feigned indignation. "Not another penny for you, Frank Sullivan," she said in ringing tones. "No, not another cent will you ever get out of me. Gambling and drinking it all away while your poor family suffers. Have you no shame?"

Sullivan was uneasily aware that a hostile crowd had gathered, but Mrs. Norris continued her denunciation at the top of her lungs.

"I've given you all I can spare," she shouted, "and still you hound me for more. Didn't I let you have a hundred dollars last month to buy medicine for your poor old mother? Didn't you guzzle it all up in drink while she lay sick and your children were starving? NO, Frank Sullivan, if you haven't got the gumption to do an honest day's work — "

The crowd was growing increasingly belligerent, and Sullivan turned in desperation and fled down the Avenue, followed by a chorus of boos and hisses, while Mrs. Norris smiled to herself contentedly and went on with her window-shopping.

Sullivan is capable of a little play-acting of his own. During an illness in New York, his friend Joe Bryan sent him a bottle of twelve-year-old Scotch. Weeks passed without any word of thanks, and at last Bryan, encountering him in "109" one evening, asked meekly if he'd ever received the gift. "Look, Bryan," Sullivan said testily, "I was sick. In *bed!* Do you give your sick friends twelve-year-old flowers? Do you offer them twelve-year-old candy? If you want any thanks from me, send me fresh whiskey."

For a brief period our apartment afforded refuge to a young and as yet unrecognized writer, William Faulkner. Ben Wasson, a literary agent, explained to us that his client from Oxford, Mississippi, was completing a story, and wondered whether he might work in our apartment while temporarily in the city. Faulkner proved to be a gnomelike figure, with enormous dark eyes and a tiny mustache perched precariously above an even tinier, pursed mouth. He preferred to write with his shoes and socks off, to Annie's visible annoyance, and would sit in the center of our living room pounding at a portable typewriter and occasionally ripping out a half-finished page and tossing it on the floor in disgust. Annie, the soul of neatness, would pounce on each sheet of paper as it fell and throw it into the fireplace. I hesitate to think what those discarded pages might be worth to a collector today. When he left, our grateful guest took down a copy of *The Sound and the Fury* from my bookshelf, and autographed the flyleaf: "Corey Ford's book is hereby presented to Frank Sullivan with the regards of Wm. Faulkner." Sullivan never gave it back to me, either.

Friends were always dropping in at 433 to while away an evening at the Word Game, the origin of Knock Knock, in which a player informs the group "I can give you a sentence

William Faulkner by Covarrubias. From *In the Worst Possible Taste.*

with" and then names a word such as Sanctuary ("Sanctuary much") or Eskimo, Christians, Italian ("Eskimo Christians Italian no lies") or F.P.A.'s Meretricious ("I wish you a meretricious and a happy New Year"). An even more popular indoor sport in those days was charades, and we spent long hours acting out political slogans and book titles and well-known songs. The longest of the hours was spent by Heywood Broun, who described in his slow deliberate drawl a very large yak in a zoo which, after several thousand words of description, got up to its feet. When nobody could guess what song title it was, Broun told us triumphantly, "Mighty yak arose." Marc Connelly, a born actor, went into an elaborate production to illustrate another title, and was happily dramatizing the second syllable of his charade when Crouse guessed the answer. Connelly glared at him. "You *spoiled* it," he said sulkily.

So great was the parlor-game craze in the Twenties that Viking Press brought out a question book called *Ask Me Another*. To arouse added interest, the editors tested the questions in advance on various celebrities, so that the reader could compare his own I.Q. (usually favorably) with the ratings of Carl Van Doren, Grantland Rice, the Lunts, and other victims. These sample tests were conducted by George Oppenheimer, playwright and critic and a Viking editor. When he visited our apartment, Sullivan and I tried to help each other out by coaching in pantomime behind our interrogator's back, but both of us flunked miserably. To console us, Oppenheimer reported that he had recently tested George Kaufman on Geography, a subject which bored him thoroughly. When asked "What is the longest river in South America?" Kaufman pondered a moment, and then countered, "Are you sure it's in South America?"

Beatrice Kaufman, George's brilliant wife, was assigned the equally dull subject of Famous Authors. To the first question, "Who wrote *The Virginian?*", she answered wearily, "Owen

Wister." Oppenheimer's second question was "Who wrote *The Virginians?*" Mrs. Kaufman replied with mounting irritation, "Owens Wisters."

During the years we lived together, I spent much of my time commuting between New York and the town of Freedom, New Hampshire, where I had bought an old farm and built a stone house. There was an orchard on the farm with a good supply of Baldwin apples, which are deceptively red but hard as rocks, and that fall I shipped a crate of them down to the apartment for Annie to use in cooking. The crate arrived the evening before I returned, and as I walked into the apartment early the following morning I saw a complete picture-without-words. The crate was on the kitchen table, a single slat had been removed, and the slat and a hammer rested side by side. One apple had been taken out of the crate, one bite had been taken out of the apple, both the bite and the remainder of the apple were on the table, and Sullivan had gone to bed. Along about noon he showed up in my room, clad in a bathrobe, and after some preliminary sparring I asked him if he had seen the crate of apples. He nodded. "Those apples are from my farm," I told him.

"Your farm is better off without them," he snarled, wrapped his robe around him, and stalked out of the room.

Sometimes it seemed to me that I fell halfway between two decades, too young for the present one and too old for the next. The generation I belonged to would not make itself felt for another ten years; whereas the members of the Round Table were of a generation ten years ahead of me. I was like a precocious child at a grown-ups' party, and could sense a slight embarrassment when they talked to me, as though they were trying to think of something appropriate to say like, "Well, well, and how have you been doing in your studies?" To make it worse, I had one of those innocuous baby faces which blushed easily, making me look even less than my middle twenties. Butlers with trays of cocktails would hesitate, uncertain whether to serve me a drink, and once a reporter who came to the apartment to interview me asked if my father was home. Sullivan, ten years my senior, used to sigh, "Oh, Ford, to be your age and know what I know now."

I tagged along with him to the gatherings of the clan at Neysa McMein's studio or at George and Beatrice Kaufman's brownstone house on East Sixty-third Street, and he would introduce me as his little nephew just down from prep school for the weekend. All the other guests had long since established their professional reputations, all orbited in the same inner circle, and I would stand ill-at-ease amid their private laughter, while my eyes moved fascinated over the awesome assemblage: Ethel Barrymore, George Gershwin, Harpo Marx, Helen Hayes, Ring Lardner, Edna Ferber. Zelda and Scott Fitzgerald, looking like two romantic characters out of one of Scott's own novels. Beatrice Kaufman, seating herself on a cane-bottomed chair which collapsed under her, leaving her trapped with her feet in the air. "If I've told you once, I've told you a thousand times," F.P.A. said to her sternly, "that's not funny." Don Stewart and his lovely wife Bea. She was pregnant at the time (last Christmas Day Don had optimistically given her a receipted reservation at the Maternity Hospital for the following September 25) and liked to leave a party early. "Don," I heard her whisper as midnight approached, "would you do me a favor — ?" "But, darling," he protested, "I thought I already had."

George Kaufman was always alone in the crowd, tall and gaunt, his hair brushed up in a high pompadour, a pair of tortoise-shell glasses riding well down on his nose, his eyes fixed on some invisible object on the ceiling. His fierce predatory look made headwaiters and taxi drivers quail; though actually he was painfully shy. He had an inspired gift for puns. "One man's Mede is another man's Persian" was one of his best known. During a weekly poker game at the Algonquin, he gazed bleakly at a poor hand and exclaimed, "I have been tray-deuced." One night, having sat for three hours on a hard wooden plank at the Greenwich Village Theater while covering an O'Neill opening, he complained in his *Times* review: "The benches should be covered by a long felt want." And he was said to have jolted the usually imperturbable producer, Jed Harris, who had a habit of disconcerting clients by receiving them in his bedroom stark naked. Kaufman entered the room and blinked at the small hairy figure on the bed. "Pardon me," he murmured politely, "your fly is open."

On Sundays our parties circled nearer home to the apartment of our neighbor Alexander Woollcott, who lived only a block away. Woollcott's books had prospered, he had signed a lucrative radio contract as "The Town Crier," and in 1929 he moved into the Campanile, a cooperative residential building at Fifty-second Street and the East River, which also housed his close friends Alice Duer Miller and Ralph and Peggy Pulitzer. He cogitated long and profitably (it gave him material for several magazine pieces) on a proper name for his new domicile. After some thought, he rejected "Atrocious Manor" and "Old Manse River," and settled for Dorothy Parker's "Wit's End." This matter disposed of, he issued formal invitations to a linen-china-and-silver shower. The literal F.P.A. arrived with a handkerchief, a mustache cup, and a silver dime. Mrs. Parker, ever thoughtful, brought a paper bag full of garbage to make the place more homey. Since Woollcott had no garbage pail, there was a problem of where to put it. Benchley suggested using the bed, but Mrs. Parker demurred. "That," she said, "is the coward's way out."

"Wit's End" was the scene of Woollcott's grueling Sunday

breakfasts, to which his friends flocked each week for the privilege of being heckled by their host. His apartment was on the first floor, with a large living-room window looking directly onto the river; and Woollcott always sat with his back to the window, silhouetted against the glaring light, clad in red silk pajamas with his legs crossed and his large paunch straining at the coat buttons to provide a glimpse of a dimpling navel: for all the world like an enormous and slightly obscene Buddha. From this vantage point, he could hurl his barbs at will around the room. Dear old Aleck spared no effort to make each new arrival uncomfortable. When Russel Crouse showed up wearing a violently chromatic shirt, Woollcott's eyes lit on it with relish. "What I admire most about Crouse," he told the assembled guests, "is his loyalty." Crouse cringed, bracing himself for the blow. "Here he is a busy author and columnist and playwright," he continued, "and still he takes the time to go all the way back to that little Army and Navy store in Skaneateles, New York, to buy his shirts."

One of my Sunday visits coincided with the publication of a John Riddell parody of Kathleen Norris and her husband, based on Charles G.'s recent tract about birth control called *Seed,* in which I suggested — with what Woollcott termed my gossamer touch — that Mrs. Norris should practice book control, since her last dozen novels had been born weak and all died. As I entered Woollcott's living room, momentarily blinded by the reflection from the river, I saw my host gesture me toward a vacant chair: "Sit right there, Ford." Gradually my eyes adjusted themselves, and I discovered that I was located between Kathleen and Charles G. Norris. To Woollcott's vast glee, they ignored me pointedly and I consumed my meal in silence, a sensation akin to eating a picnic lunch between the two stone lions in front of the Public Library.

Woollcott was high priest of the Cult of Rudeness, perfected at the Round Table — the Vicious Circle, the group called themselves — where abuse was the accepted form of conversation; and his extraordinary vocabulary made his insults cut like a surgeon's scalpel. Sighting Neysa McMein arriving at a party in a spangled evening gown, he hailed her across the room: "Neysa, you're scrofulous with mica." He took pride in pinning his victims dead center, but he relished as much being on the receiving end of a riposte. It delighted him no end when a critic compared him to a butterfly in heat, or when Howard Dietz, fed up with Woollcott's oft-repeated references to *Little Women,* insisted on calling him Louisa M. Woollcott. His fondness for Dietz dated from a backgammon game during which they became involved in a loud argument. "Are you trying to cross me, Dietz?" Woollcott challenged. "I wouldn't cross you with an alpenstock," Dietz retorted.

He was just as pleased when Frank Sullivan gave him his comeuppance. Woollcott had returned recently from a successful lecture tour through the Middle West, and informed his friends a trifle pompously, "I spoke to ten thousand women in St. Paul."

"What did you tell them?" Sullivan inquired. " 'No'?"

His hunched shoulders, his beaked nose, his eyes glinting behind the great round frames of his spectacles gave the impression of a malevolent owl, waiting for a heedless mouse to stray across his path. Unlike other Round Table regulars, his witticisms were unrehearsed. At a Sunday brunch, he noticed an unusual barge coming down the East River, and interrupted the conversation to ask Junior, his colored servant, "What kind of craft is that?" Junior glanced out the window, and replied, "It's a Standard Oil tanker." "You're welcome," Woollcott said, and resumed his conversation.

To help reduce — he was very conscious of his weight — he acquired a steam cabinet with a glass window in front. Peggy

Pulitzer, wandering through the apartment one afternoon, happened to glance through the cabinet window and saw Woollcott seated inside, totally nude. She gave a little squeal and retreated to the living room, and when Woollcott finished his bath and joined her, she suggested, "Really, Aleck, you should cover that window with an organdy curtain."

"Curtain de organ," he corrected her.

One of his favorite diversions was to startle a friend with the announcement that he was about to descend on him for a specified number of days, and demand certain household arrangements in that imperious manner which Kaufman and Hart mocked in their play about Woollcott, *The Man Who Came to Dinner.* Sullivan averted an impending visit to his family home in Saratoga by warning him, "We have only one bathroom, so you'll have to take pot luck." I was not so agile. Sullivan and I were sitting in the Men's Bar at the Ritz when Woollcott paused beside our table, fixed me with his glittering eye, and announced, "Ford, I plan to spend three days at your house in New Hampshire next week." The prospect of entertaining such a demanding guest in my modest home was terrifying, but I managed to stammer out a weak "Gee, Aleck, that will be swell." "I'll be the judge of that," Woollcott retorted, and swept toward the door, with a private wink at Sullivan.

His prose was so gushing and effusive, when he was carried away by one of his schoolgirl crushes over Minnie Maddern Fiske or *Goodbye, Mr. Chips,* that George Jean Nathan termed him "The Seidlitz Powder of Broadway"; but his ornate style was not the result of any conscious effort. Rather, polysyllabic words came so naturally that, when he dictated a radio script, he had to rewrite it so that it would not sound affected. It was a hard style to imitate, as I learned when I attempted a *Vanity Fair* parody:

When your effervescent correspondent, *skippity hop,* has had his last fit of the vapors and toddled into his anecdotage, *skippity hop, skippity hop,* and the tittering group of old meanies gather around the so-styled Round Table at that excellent inn in the Forties, *knit one, purl one,* where he used to regale the gaping (right in his face, Master Connelly claims) throng with the steaming gossip and motley bubble, *shame, shame, tell your beau's name,* of that period which Master Adams suggests might be known henceforth as the Slightly Decay'd, *now I am on my roller skates and going like sixty,* which he once collected in a lilac-haunted, *faster, faster,* Memory Book called (*look out, the end of the page is dead ahead*) "Going to, *whee, here I come,* Pieces," BAM!

It was inevitable that his arrogant air and adder tongue would arouse resentment — and it must be said that no one was quicker than Woollcott himself to resent an imagined or unintentional slight — and he was constantly involved in feuds with his friends. One of the most bitter was with Edna Ferber, a lady of great wit and asperity, who denounced him as "that New Jersey Nero, wearing his pinafore like a toga and fiddling while Rome burns." Woollcott promptly seized Miss Ferber's phrase "While Rome Burns" and made it the title of his most successful collection, which went through fifteen printings in its first year.

There has been a tendency in recent years to downgrade Woollcott, and dismiss him as a dilettante and churl. Possibly this stems from his on-and-off feud with Harold Ross. Ross never took the quarrel seriously (their friendship dated back to the days they served together on *Stars and Stripes* in World War I) but the younger writers on *The New Yorker* worshiped Ross and rallied loyally to his defense. James Thurber, in *The Years with Ross,* was less than kind to Woollcott, and Wolcott Gibbs's three-part Profile in *The New Yorker* called "Big Nemo" made tasteless references to Woollcott's mincing and precious manner, and cast doubts on his masculinity. (Actually Woollcott had been rendered sterile by an attack of mumps when a boy.) Granted he was vain and overbearing; but his abusive front masked a basic dependence on his friends, and he was capable of great thoughtfulness and sympathy. Margalo Gillmore summed him up as "deadly cutting and marvelously kind," and that will do till a better appraisal comes to hand.

It was Gibbs's vindictive Profile which brought about the final break with Ross. Woollcott never spoke to him again. Once, after a heart attack, he wrote Ross and suggested a reconciliation for old times' sake; but he began to feel better and withdrew his offer. Woollcott died suddenly during a radio broadcast, in the midst of an insult he was delivering over the air: vituperative and lonely to the end.

# 7

## The Making of a Magazine

IN 1924, my first year out of college, I was finding it hard
sledding to subsist on the short humor articles I was selling
to *Life,* and so I did an occasional piece for its rival magazine
*Judge.* The pay was small, and slow in coming, but I was
strongly drawn to *Judge*'s new editor, Harold W. Ross, who
had just been moved over from the *American Legion Weekly*
in one of those publishing upheavals of the Twenties. Actually
he was co-editor; the other half of the editorial chair was
occupied by Norman Anthony, whose merry monkey-face would
fold into innumerable wrinkles when he doubled with laughter.

Ross seldom laughed aloud. If something amused him, his
upper body heaved spasmodically a couple of times, and his
heavy lips parted in a broad silent grin, showing large teeth
with a gap in the center. He wore his coarse brown hair brushed
upright to a height of three inches; and now and then, when he
was embarrassed or frustrated, he would rub a hand across his
face and comb his fingers back through the thatch of hair in one
prolonged gesture of confusion, or explode with a heartfelt
"Jesus!" and then grin at his own ineptness.

It is hard to say what inspired my immediate confidence in

him. He looked like a bucolic bumpkin, his features plain to the point of being homely, his big hands flailing in all directions to bolster his inarticulate speech. Often he would leave a sentence unfinished, and fling both arms aloft in utter futility. He was always perched on the edge of his chair, ready to leap up and start pacing the room in restless pursuit of an idea. Even when standing in one spot, he managed to remain in motion, jangling a pocketful of keys and loose change or stabbing the air with a forefinger or banging the desk as his voice rose to a squawk: "This goddam place is driving me bughouse." His language was a curious admixture of roundhouse oaths and bits of antiquated slang which dated back to my earliest boyhood: bughouse, spooning, stuck on her, sis. After a tirade, his mobile face would light with sheepish amusement and he would sigh, "God, how I pity me." It was his balancing sense of humor about himself, I think, that made him a great editor, another of the half-dozen greatest I've known. "All right, Ford," he would conclude with a limp wave of his hand. "God bless you."

*Judge* had been skidding badly when Ross was called in. Its format was a hodgepodge, its editorial contents catered to the lowest level of readership with "Krazy Kracks" purchased for five dollars a krack, and outrageous puns called "Funnybones" printed inside silhouettes of dog bones. Contributors were never paid till after publication, and then only when they threatened a lawsuit. Ross, who championed his writers and artists, pleaded with the business department for better and more prompt remuneration; but the magazine's advertising had dwindled almost to nothing, and he stormed and ranted in vain.

He felt he knew the reason for *Judge*'s financial woes. One day I brought in an article about New York's snow-removal problems, and Ross had to turn it down because its appeal was too limited for a national circulation. "That's the trouble with this goddam magazine," he squawked, striding up and down his office. "If it went after a local audience, it would get local advertising." He glared at me as though it were my fault. "Why should a New York restaurant or theater or perfume shop spend money for an ad that would be wasted on the rest of the country? There's enough revenue right here in this city to support a smart metropolitan weekly." He carried his argument to the top, but the publishers laughed at him. Their inflexible attitude convinced him (if he ever needed convincing) that the editorial department of a magazine should be rigidly independent of the business office, a policy which he followed on *The New Yorker* to such a degree that the departments were housed in separate buildings two blocks apart.

The idea of a sophisticated humorous weekly about Manhattan had been in his mind since the war. It should be topical, he felt, and printed as speedily as a newspaper so that its comments would be timely. He insisted that there would be no "bedroom stuff," another of his quaint expressions. "Every magazine I pick up has a man carrying a woman off to bed. There'll be no, by God, sex in this one." (Sometimes, if ladies were present, he spelled it out S-E-X.) Three decades later, in his obit in *The New Yorker* after Ross's death, E. B. White wrote: "His dream was a simple dream; it was pure and had no frills: he wanted the magazine to be good, to be funny, and to be fair."

Realizing that his hands were tied at *Judge,* he resigned his job to gamble everything on the simple dream. With his wife, Jane Grant, he made up a tentative dummy and showed it hopefully at lunch at the Algonquin. Franklin P. Adams and Alexander Woollcott, both of whom had served with him overseas on the staff of *Stars and Stripes,* were not impressed. Although Ross was liked by the Round Table group, its members did not take him seriously, and his raffish face and gawky manner made him the butt of continual "joshing," as he called

it. Woollcott, who considered Ross his personal protégé, described him as "a dishonest Abe Lincoln," and Ina Claire
expressed a desire to take off her shoes and wade through his
hair. (The remark got around, and Ross had the barber flatten
his pompadour at once.) One winter F.P.A. invited him to
Connecticut for a healthful weekend coasting on the snow, and
on Monday someone asked how Ross had looked tobogganing.
Adams threw back his head, parted his lips with an audible
smack, and closed both eyes in his characteristic attitude of
thought. "Well," he replied, "you know how he looks *not*
tobogganing." None of the Vicious Circle dreamed that his
magazine would be one of the most phenomenal successes in
publishing history, and they scoffed at the idea of sinking
money in his venture.

Ross found a backer at last in Raoul Fleischmann, whose
family had amassed a tidy fortune in the baking business.
"You've heard that thirteen loaves make a baker's dozen,"
Fleischmann said once to Joe Bryan. "Well, our family made it
eleven." He was attracted to creative people, and the prospect of
financing a magazine of wit and sophistication appealed to him,
particularly when Ross, with wild impracticality, estimated that
an investment of fifty thousand would be enough to put it over.
(Fleischmann was to sink $710,000 over the next three years
until the magazine came out of the red.) Late that summer of
1924, Ross set up his offices at 25 West 45th Street, in a building owned by Fleischmann. His sole editorial assistants were
Tip Bliss, a humor writer and veteran of the *Stars and Stripes,*
and a public relations man named Philip Wylie, so young and
frail that Marc Connelly mistook him for an office boy. The
only professional around the office was the debonair and immensely capable Rea Irvin, former art editor of *Life,* who
dropped in one day a week to look over the illustrations and
cartoons.

Still the magazine was without a name, and to stimulate interest Ross offered a reward of fifteen hundred dollars in stock for the best suggestion. John Peter Toohey, a theatrical press agent, was lunching at the Round Table and overheard the subject being discussed. He looked up from his plate. "What kind of a magazine is it supposed to be?" he asked idly. "A magazine about New York," someone told him. "Then call it *The New Yorker*," Toohey said, and returned to his meal. In view of the present value of *New Yorker* stock, those were probably the highest paying three words on record. Fired with excitement, Ross promptly hammered out a prospectus, unique among editorial manifestos, with a concluding paragraph which has become a byword:

> *The New Yorker* will be the magazine which is not edited for the old lady in Dubuque. It will not be concerned in what she is thinking about. This is not meant in disrespect, but *The New Yorker* is a magazine avowedly published for a metropolitan audience, and thereby will escape an influence which hampers most national publications. It expects a considerable national circulation, but this will come from persons who have a metropolitan interest.

Fleischmann felt that the magazine needed window-dressing, and asked Ross to list some celebrated names on the masthead as Advisory Editors. After polling the Round Table, he chose Ralph Barton, Marc Connelly, Edna Ferber, Rea Irvin, George S. Kaufman, Alice Duer Miller, Dorothy Parker, and Alexander Woollcott. Though Miss Ferber was fond of Ross, she withdrew from the board because she did not want to be connected with a failure. F.P.A. and Heywood Broun were under contract to the *World* and therefore unavailable, and Benchley and Sherwood, both on *Life,* could scarcely be publicly associated with a rival publication. After several months Woollcott, sensing a sinking ship, demanded that his name be removed, a severe blow to the morale of the staff. The meaning-less board of Advisory Editors was dropped from the masthead at the end of the year, to Ross's immense relief. "Most dis-honest thing I ever did," he confessed later.

The first issue of *The New Yorker* appeared on February 21, 1925, and was, to put it gently, a disappointment. The hand-some cover by Rea Irvin, depicting a top-hatted dandy peering through his monocle at a butterfly, has appeared on every anniversary issue since; but the rest of the magazine bore little or no resemblance to *The New Yorker* of today. It started with a department entitled "Of All Things," obviously patterned on *Punch*'s famous Charivari but which failed to capture the urban-ity and wit of its British model. This was followed by "The Talk of the Town," a collection of anecdotes written in the first person and signed in longhand "Van Bibber III." There was a tattle column in the style of small-town newspapers called "In Our Midst," an innocuous Profile of Gatti-Casazza written by "Golly-wogg" (drama critic Gilbert Gabriel) and illustrated by Covarrubias, and short bits by F.P.A., Fairfax Downey, and Arthur H. Folwell, former editor of *Puck*. My own offering was an arty vignette of Manhattan, in fragmentary phrases linked with trailing dots, something the present *New Yorker* would never dream of printing. Ralph Barton drew a rather gruesome caricature for the drama section, Wallace Morgan contributed a center spread in the stereotyped *Life* tradition, and Al Frueh was represented by a full-page cartoon showing the effect on a nervous household of a painting of the Leaning Tower of Pisa, which would have fitted as well in *Judge*. To parody the routine two-line jokes of the comic magazines, Ross reversed an old chestnut to read: *"Pop:* A man who thinks he can make it in par. *Junior:* What is an optimist, Pop?"; but the point was somewhat dulled by the presence of several conventional two-liners in the same issue. The layout was rococo and jumbled, the headings too large and the print so small that it was difficult to read, and the old lady in Dubuque was not the only one who found it unappealing.

Ross went to work in frantic haste to improve his magazine. In the second issue, "The Talk of the Town" (still in the first person and signed "Van Bibber III") led off the book, which was highlighted by a Dorothy Parker essay on a typical club-woman. The third issue had a Profile by Woollcott (unsigned) and "The Talk of the Town" dropped back to page 13; but the next issue found it once more in its original spot, and Van Bibber's name disappeared forever. For the most part, the contents were undistinguished, and Ross's friends at the Algonquin were slow to rally to his aid. Mrs. Parker, who had promised faithfully to come to the office after lunch and write an article, was discovered by Ross later that afternoon sitting in Tony's. "I'm sorry," she explained, "but someone was using the pencil." Edna Ferber's Profile of William Allen White was her only contribution that first critical year; Frank Sullivan's total effort was limited to three pieces; Benchley was ten months getting around to writing anything; Ring Lardner submitted a solitary article in 1925; Marc Connelly and Gluyas Williams were not represented until the following year; and George Kaufman's name appeared for the first time in 1935.

Unable to count on his friends during that period of travail, Ross beat the bush for newcomers. Curtis Arnoux Peters, Jr., a tall and talented young man recently out of Yale, took time off from playing the piano for Gilda Grey to try some comic drawings which he signed Peter Arno. Helen Hokinson, a small shy unknown, submitted a sketch showing a salesgirl offering a phial of perfume to a plump customer and explaining: *It's N'Aimez Que Moi, madam — don't love nobody but me.* It was the start of Hoky's unforgettable series of middle-aged suburban housewives and garden clubbers, one of the magazine's best-loved features. Early in May, Lois Long left *Vanity Fair* to take over a department called "When Nights Are Bold," later changed to "Tables for Two," and the popular signature "Lipstick" made its first appearance in *The New Yorker*. That same momentous issue of May 9, 1925, carried a small essay entitled "Defense of the Bronx River," signed with the initials E.B.W. In his sensitive and limpid style, Elwyn Brooks White wrote tenderly of the little stream that "rises in Valhalla and flows south to Hell Gate":

Commuters on the New Haven and the Central know the Bronx, they know it of old by reputation, and of late by name. And they stand up for it. In Spring the willows along the shore turn a pleasant yellow, and the stream takes their color, and the little tributaries of the Bronx come rushing down from the hills in pipes and empty into the main stream, augmenting it and causing white rapids at Bedford Park. I have seen commuters forsake their newspaper and flatten their nose on the window as the train glided along the Bronx River. And I have seen a strange light come into their eyes, especially if there was a duck or something like that floating on the water. And here is one commuter who wouldn't trade this elegant little river, with its ducks and rapids and pipes and commissions, and willows, for the Amazon or the Snohomish or LaPlatte or the Danube, or the Mississippi, even though the latter does rise in Lake Itaska and flow south to the Gulf of Mexico, and is wider.

Ross's instinct must have told him that here was the indefinable formula he had been groping for, that E. B. White's quality of rueful humor would give *The New Yorker* the prestige he desired; and it was ironic to think that the discovery might have come too late. His magazine was wasting away before his eyes. Circulation had dropped to less than ten thousand, returned copies were stacked high in the mail room, and the average issue was down to twenty-four pages. Advertising was so scanty that he could not sell the space inside the front cover, telltale sign of a terminal sickness. On May 9, as the issue with White's first article hit the stands, Fleischmann informed a grim luncheon group that he was pulling out.

Only one thing saw *The New Yorker* through its darkest hour, and that was Ross himself. He had been toughened by his early years as a tramp newspaperman, riding freights and bumming meals in the West; he had resiliency and unconquerable enthusiasm; he was not about to give up. He and Fleischmann met again that afternoon at F.P.A.'s wedding reception, and over a glass of champagne, infected by Ross's optimism, Fleischmann agreed to give the magazine another financial transfusion and keep it alive just a little longer.

The immediate problem was to fill that gaping hole on the inside front cover. Ross recalled a random series I had been writing (and illustrating, by the way) on the Fugitive Art of Manhattan: beards and mustaches on subway ads, chalked sketches on brick walls, doodles on Wall Street blotters, and the like. In his impulsive way, he called me into his office and began jangling coins and pacing the floor. Could I do a series of promotion ads to fill the goddam inside cover? Rea Irvin thought I might burlesque those house organ brochures about publishing a magazine. Have the first one by tomorrow? Done and done. God bless you.

"The Making of a Magazine," which ran for twenty issues, took the reader on a tour of the vast organization of *The New Yorker,* explaining every aspect of its production from the plantation in Mexico, which produced the cactus spines used in binding the pages together, to the Punctuation Farm where commas were raised in profusion to satisfy Ross's ravenous desire. In one issue I depicted the huge forests in Canada where trees were grown for paper; in the next issue, having discovered that the best paper is made from rags, I threw 2,001,093 paper-

jacks out of work and described instead the sunlit factory at
Niagara Falls where 3700 dressmakers were employed to manu-
facture gowns which another trained staff of 5000 girls put on
and wore in subway crushes until they were rags. There was the
Initial Department, where letters were sent to be capitalized; the
Emphasis Department which placed words in a vise and bent
them sideways into italics; and the Margin and Open Space
Department, to which carloads of open spaces were shipped
daily from sixty thousand acres owned by *The New Yorker* in
Montana and Wyoming. Ink was obtained from a Deep-Sea
Squid Farm in the Sargasso Sea, where squids were insulted
until they lost their tempers and squirted black fluid into
conveniently placed inkwells.

*The New Yorker*'s man-of-all-work, who personally super-
vised all these departments, was Mr. Eustace Tilley. ("Tilley"
was the name of a maiden aunt, and I chose "Eustace" because
it sounded euphonious.) In Johan Bull's illustrations, he appeared as a silk-hat dude, with morning coat and striped
trousers and a monocle, based on the figure in Rea Irvin's anniversary cover. In time Irvin's creation became known as Eustace
Tilley, and "Our Man Tilley" showed up now and then in the
"Talk" section. Ross even listed a private telephone under
Tilley's name. During the guerrilla war between *The New
Yorker* and the Luce publications, *Time* appropriated Eustace
Tilley as a member of its own editorial staff, but he was hastily
dropped when Ross threatened suit for plagiarism.

After seven weeks inside the front cover, the Crillon Restaurant bought the space for a full-page ad, and "The Making of a
Magazine" was evicted to the rear of the book, where it
remained ready to leap back to its former position in an
emergency. It was required only once more. Business was
picking up, as Ross's elusive dream began to take shape.
White's matchless touch brightened the "Notes and Comments"

Harold Ross as Eustace Tilley by Al Hirschfeld.

section which now led off "The Talk of the Town," mostly
written by Russel Crouse. John Held, Jr., developed a new style
(Ross had refused to use his too familiar flappers) of pseudo-
primitive linoleum blocks illustrating old ballads, such as
"Frankie and Johnny" or "Let 16 Gamblers Carry My Coffin."
Ben Hecht and Benchley and Sherwood started writing casuals,
as Ross called them, and Gene Tunney did a caricature of
George Luks. Peter Arno hit his stride with a couple of un-
disciplined old harridans, wearing long dresses and old-
fashioned crinkly hats and carrying muffs, who crashed fashionable wedding parties or glided arm-in-arm on roller-skates or
hitched rides on the rear bumpers of cars, while carrying on an
improbable dialogue ("Oh, Lordy!" "Whoops!" "I thought I'd
*die!*") which earned them the nickname of the "Whoops
Sisters." One cartoon showed the two crones seated in a bucket
at the end of a swinging crane, convulsed with laughter:

> "Whoops! Generous I calls it — free ride an' everything! More
> excitin', though, if Harry'd come along with us."
> "Lordy! It wouldn't be safe with *him* here!"
> "Lawsey, no! He was bad enough at Coney Island — Whoops!"

Circulation boomed with Ellin Mackay's sensational (for the
Twenties) attack on high society called "Why We Go to
Cabarets: A Post-Debutante Explains"; and *The New Yorker*
received further unexpected publicity when Miss Mackay, defying society and her wealthy father, eloped with a former
Bowery saloon piano player named Izzy Baline, who had
changed his name to Irving Berlin. The smart set was beginning
to take notice. Late in October Morris Markey initiated a new
department of newspaper criticism called "The Current Press"
(later it became "The Wayward Press" when Robert Benchley
wrote it under the nom de plume "Guy Fawkes") and the same

issue introduced another *New Yorker* perennial, the "Paris Letter" by Janet ("Genêt") Flanner. Local advertisers hastened to climb aboard the bandwagon; just before Christmas, B. Altman & Company agreed to purchase fifty-two pages of advertising in 1926, and Saks Fifth Avenue signed a similar contract. By January the average issue numbered forty-eight pages, double the May total. Ross's stubborn belief in a metropolitan weekly was proving sound.

As his troubles grew less, Ross could devote more time to worrying about them. The crisis had passed, his magazine was off and running, and he settled down into the distracted and harassed figure which became a *New Yorker* legend. "Why does everything happen to me?" he would lament with a martyred expression. "I'm surrounded by women and children. Nobody knows how to run this goddam place efficiently." Managing editors were hired and fired so fast that Ross lost track of them. *The New Yorker* office was a constant bedlam. If carpenters weren't hammering up partitions to satisfy the editor's sudden whim, he was busy altering the phone system or devising a new and more complicated way to route copy. He was into everything, complaining about a missing comma, filling a galley with black-penciled queries like "Who he?" and "clarify," or disrupting an art meeting by pointing to a submitted cartoon and asking, "Where am *I* supposed to be standing?" or "Which elephant is talking?" He was a perfectionist, nagging, fretting, demanding, raking his fingers through his hair and pawing the air in a frenetic quest of the ultimate, the issue without a flaw. One night at "109" Sullivan overheard him telling Benchley, "Don't think I'm not incoherent."

Whether through intuition, or persistence, or sheer blind luck, he gathered about him the nucleus of an extraordinary group of editors who would perpetuate his magazine. Some six months after *The New Yorker* started, he enlisted the services of Mrs. Katharine S. Angell, a poised and cultured lady who had written for the *Atlantic* and the *New Republic,* and whose creative mind and cool perceptive judgment balanced Ross's impetuous brilliance. Early in 1926 she recommended that he hire E. B. White, whom she subsequently married. More than anyone else save Ross himself, Katharine S. and E. B. White were responsible for *The New Yorker*'s enormous impact on American letters. Their unerring taste guided it through the formative years, and White's poetry-in-prose became the hall-mark of the magazine. Marc Connelly said, "He brought it steel and fire."

White was quiet and inward-looking, attuned to the delicate vibrations of the city, and I had read his occasional essays about Manhattan with genuine wonder and worship. He was also extremely diffident, though I did not know it at the time, uneasy with strangers and distressed at any public outburst of praise. When Ross introduced us one afternoon, I grasped his hand and assured him that in my opinion he was the finest stylist in America (an opinion I still hold). White winced perceptibly, withdrew his hand, and dematerialized through the door. Ross whirled on me indignantly. "You *sca-a-ared* him," he snarled.

Today White's preeminent position in American humor is assured. In a recent citation, the National Institute of Arts and Letters called him "the owner of an uncommon sense that is lit by laughter. . . . If we are remembered as a civilized era, it will be partly because of E. B. White. The historians of the future will decide that a writer of such grace and control could not have been produced by a generation wholly lacking in such qualities, and we will shine by reflection in his gentle light." No other writer possesses his ability to find the precise and only word: the pigeon "compact" on its nest, the grave of a pig to be revisited "in seasons of reflection and despair, on flagless memorial days of our own choosing." His weekly Notes and Comments in *The New Yorker* dealt with everything from

Professor Piccard in a balloon to Dorothy Lamour in a sarong, from the praying mantis to crabgrass and the disappearing American Home:

Housemaking reared its chintzey little head the other day when the ladies of the American Home Economics Association decided that maybe the Home should rate a Cabinet position, to be called the Department of the American Home. It is a noble idea and would unquestionably attract the wrong people. If we had a Secretary of the Home, like a Secretary of State or a Secretary of Commerce, she would probably be a lady whose emphasis would be upon vitamins and lampshades. She would be against mice. The American Home, given Cabinet status, would continue to move (as it has moved in the last few years) in the wrong direction. The American Kitchen would become more and more stagy and unlivable; the American Cellar would finally and forever emerge as a rumpus room, above ground; the Home as a whole would tend to become collapsible, transparent, mobile, washable, sterile, and devoid of human life.

In his preface to *A Subtreasury of American Humor,* edited by the Whites, he had his modest say about humor writing and humor appreciation:

The world likes humor, but it treats it patronizingly. It decorates its serious artists with laurel, and its wags with Brussels Sprouts. It feels that if a thing is funny it can be presumed to be something less than great, because if it were truly great it would be wholly serious. . . . I'm sure there isn't a humorist alive but can recall the day . . . when someone he loved and respected took him anxiously into a corner and asked him when he was "going to write something serious." That day is memorable, for it gives a man pause to realize that the bright star he is following is held to be not of the first magnitude.

For years E. B. White was largely responsible for the cartoon captions (*"It's broccoli, dear." "I say it's spinach, and I say the*

*"It's broccoli, dear."*
*"I say it's spinach, and I say the hell with it."*

Drawing by Carl Rose, caption by E. B. White; © 1928,
1956 The New Yorker Magazine, Inc.

*hell with it"* ) and the little fillers called newsbreaks which give
*The New Yorker* a special luster.* His facile mind invented
such titles as "Raised Eyebrows Department" and "Neatest
Trick of the Week," and his wry comments under the news-
breaks sounded the death knell of the two-line jokes with which
*Life* and *Judge* used to fill their space. A few samples:

> A stray dog with the name of E. G. Caldwell has been
> about the village for a few days. — *Carroll County
> (N.H.) Independent.*
> *Not old Eddy Caldwell?*

> Mr. and Mrs. Frank Di Pietro, of Miles Avenue, are
> receiving congratulations on the birth of their daughter.
> Both mother and baby are doing nicely under the car of
> Dr. Robert Sievers. — *Bordentown (N.J.) Register.*
> *That animal instinct to go where it's quiet and dark.*

> I tell those aspiring writers who write me for advice to
> read, read, read. Everything. From the classical writers to
> the modern. Write, write, write tirelessly, all the time.
> Then, above all, one must have lived. — *Louis Bromfield,
> interviewed in The Writer.*
> *Have lived, have lived, have lived!*

> LOST — Male fox hound, brown head, yellow legs, blue
> body with large black spots on left side, male. Also female,
> white with red head and spot on hip. — *Fayette (Mo.)
> Democrat-Leader.*
> *Those aren't dogs, those are nasturtiums.*

---

* After reading the manuscript of this chapter, White wrote: "It would,
I fear, be an exaggeration to say that for years I was responsible for the cartoon captions. I was simply a cartoon doctor. I was given drawings that were
hanging around the shop waiting for a better caption, or a fix. These were
a small part of the whole. The broccoli drawing came in with a caption that
had no resemblance to the one I gave it. On the other hand, it's an *under-
statement* to say that "for years" I was responsible for the newsbreaks. Hell,
I still do them every week. Some sort of record, I guess."

*The Lyrical Press*
There is still no news of the party of Jews who left
Portobello on Sunday. — *Manchester Guardian.*
*But we choose to think that they did not sink, and will
turn up for work on Monday.*

Late the following year Ross added two more important
names to his hard core of editors. Both Wolcott Gibbs and James
Thurber joined the staff in 1927, though Thurber's drawings of
strange dogs and stranger humans did not appear in *The New
Yorker* until after 1930. (Most of the magazine's leading
writers and artists made their first appearance in the Thirties.)
Gibbs was a thin, nervous, sometimes rancorous intellectual,
armed with a tart wit. Visiting Moss Hart's estate in Bucks
County, which had been elaborately landscaped with imported
trees and shrubs, he remarked, "It just goes to show what God
could do if he had enough money." A precisionist, Gibbs
became *The New Yorker*'s star copy editor, correcting or rewriting casuals and stories without distorting an author's style or
arousing his ire. Katharine White calls him "the best rewrite
man to salvage a piece of uncured humor." Later, when Gibbs
took over Benchley's post as drama critic, his reviews were so
caustic that producers sought to ban him from their theaters, but
Ross respected Gibbs's integrity and stood by him, and the
producers had to back down. His fine ear for parody displayed
itself in his Profile of Henry Luce, probably the most successful
of all *New Yorker* Profiles, which was written in *Time*'s
spasmodic style of reversed words ("Backward ran sentences
until reeled the mind") and concluded with the famed tag-line:
"Where it all will end, knows God."
    Ross had a paternal attitude toward his staff, but Thurber was
the object of his special solicitude, since Ross had convinced
himself that Thurber was impractical and helpless. In his

memoir, *The Years with Ross,* Thurber wrote: "If a manuscript was lost, 'Thurber lost it.' Once he accused me of losing a typescript which later turned up in a briefcase of his own. 'If it hadn't been there,' he said, 'Thurber would have lost it.' " Ross's associates had an irresistible urge to harry him, and Woollcott and Parker and Long were constantly trying to sneak double entendres into their copy. (Mrs. Parker succeeded once with the phrase "like shot through a goose.") Thurber was the prime harrier. When the carpenters were making so much noise that he couldn't work, he added to the din by rolling empty metal wastebaskets up and down the hall until Ross yelled at his secretary, "Go find out what the hell's going on, but don't tell me." One afternoon Thurber mislaid his jacket, and burst into Ross's office in the midst of a conference to protest, "Somebody stole my coat." Ross assured him it would turn up and waved him away, but a couple of minutes later Thurber reappeared, stripped to the waist. "Somebody stole my shirt, too," he complained. After an arduous staff meeting, the story goes, Thurber discovered that the carpenters had left a hall telephone booth flat on the floor, and he stretched out full length inside it, his hands folded on his breast. The pranks seem a little childish in retrospect, like pampered tots teasing Nannie; but Ross recognized them, I am sure, as a bid for attention, an indication of his staff's jealous devotion.

Ross was equally devoted to his acolytes, though he had his own way of showing it. Thurber liked to recall the day that an enraged cartoonist demanded of Ross, "Why do you reject my work and publish drawings by a fourth-rate artist like Thurber?" Ross rose loyally to Thurber's defense. "You mean a third-rate artist," he corrected. During World War II, Thurber had to undergo a series of eye operations, and Ross came to visit him in the hospital while headlines were screaming of the German blitz on London. "Goddam it, Thurber," he admitted in a rare display of emotion, "I worry about you and England."

Of the myriad books and plays and articles about Ross, no two writers have seen him the same way. Thurber's biography made him out restless, exasperating, innocent. Margaret Case Harriman, in *The Vicious Circle,* felt that "actually he was about as naïve and bewildered as Machiavelli, Gypsy Rose Lee, or the President of Standard Oil." In Gibbs's Broadway hit about Ross, *A Season in the Sun,* he was depicted as virtually a maniac, looking up the word "hurricane" in a dictionary while the winds threatened to demolish his Fire Island cottage. On the other hand, Frank Sullivan, one of his closest friends, found him wise and warm and full of humor. There was the night that Sullivan and I dined with Ross at "21" during one of his recurrent pill-nibbling periods. His doctor had put him on a strict diet, and he scanned the menu wanly for something he could eat. The waiter sought to be helpful. "How about a nice vegetable dinner?" he suggested. Ross whipped off his glasses and scowled. "That," he stated, "is a contradiction in terms." After lengthy deliberation he told the waiter, "Bring me a stewed orange." The waiter, rocked by the order, said uncertainly, "I'm afraid we don't have a stewed orange." Again the glasses were snatched off, and Ross's arm flailed in a half-circle. "Then go stew one," he growled.

Certainly no figure could have seemed less likely as the editor of the nation's most sophisticated weekly. His belligerent pompadour had been tamed, except when his combing fingers stirred it up, but he walked slouched forward, as though he were shoving something, and his clothes never quite fit. Eustace Tilley would have cut him dead on the street. He favored dark suits and ties, a subconscious instinct for camouflage. He had a passionate desire to be anonymous (a tradition loyally carried on by his shy and able successor, William Shawn) and devised elaborate schemes to enter or leave his office without being seen. (Once he toyed with the idea of cutting a staircase to the floor below.) His name appeared in *The New Yorker* for the first time in White's obit after his death in 1951. He had a particular phobia about being called on to speak in public. I remember a Columbia *Jester* banquet, at which Ross was given a surprise award as the man who had done most for humor writing. Ross lurched to his feet and grabbed the plaque, glanced wildly around the room, uttered a stricken *"Je*-sus" and sat down. Sullivan, who was seated next to him, shook his head. "Your speech was too long, Ross," he chided. "I got bored after the first syllable."

In the latter Thirties, after the disappearance of the other comic magazines, *The New Yorker* became virtually the sole custodian of American wit and humor. It was during that decade and the next — beyond the arbitrary limit I have set for this book — that the magazine reached its height with Sullivan's annual Christmas poems (which started in 1932), Clarence Day's immortal sketches of his father (dramatized by Lindsay and Crouse in *Life with Father*), and Ruth McKenney's *My Sister Eileen* (also the basis for a successful play). John O'Hara's "Pal Joey" series furnished the book for the Rodgers and Hart Broadway hit, Thurber's "The Secret Life of Walter Mitty" was widely reprinted and made into a motion picture, John Hersey's *Hiroshima* shattered precedent by taking up an entire issue, and St. Clair McKelway's six-part Profile on Walter Winchell succeeded in getting Ross barred from the Stork Club. Other noted *New Yorker* names belong to the period after the depression: Ogden Nash, Rebecca West, Alva Johnston, Nunnally Johnson, Joel Sayre, S. J. Perelman, Phyllis McGinley, Margaret Fishback, S. N. Behrman, A. J. Liebling, Lillian Ross, Arthur Kober, Clifton Fadiman. The Thirties saw the first appearance of some of *The New Yorker*'s best-known artists: Whitney Darrow, Jr., Sydney Hoff, Robert Day, Richard Taylor, Sam Cobean, Chon Day, George Price, Saul Steinberg, and Charles Addams, whose monsters introduced a new kind of black humor to the magazine. Kay Boyle pioneered the school of introspective fiction in 1931 with a short story called "Kroy Wen," the beginning of the self-analytic and pastel stories-without-plots which have become a *New Yorker* standby. Mrs. White guided their writers with sensitivity and tact, but Ross was never quite comfortable about running what he called "grim stuff." "If a man in these goddam stories doesn't shoot his wife, he shoots himself," he used to rant. "Everybody's s-l-e-e-p-i-n-g with everybody else. It's a hell of a thing, but I guess there's nothing to do about it." Despite his misgivings, stories by O'Hara, Sally Benson, Thyra Samter Winslow, Robert Coates, John Cheever, Nancy Hale, and J. D. Salinger tended to dominate *The New Yorker,* and in recent years, as humor failed to keep up the pace, fiction drew ahead. But that isn't part of my story . . .

Shortly before Ross died, John McNulty, one of his favorite writers, shared a seat with him on a commuter train to Connecticut. Ross made no mention of his malignant illness, and they talked long and sentimentally of the magazine and its memories. The train stopped at Stamford, where Ross lived, and he stood up and looked at McNulty for a moment. "All right, McNulty, God bless you, goddamit," he said, and hurried up the aisle and through the door. That blend of blasphemy and emotion was Harold Ross. "When he sent you away with this benediction, which he uttered briskly and affectionately, and in which he and God seemed all scrambled together, it carried a warmth and sincerity that never failed to carry over," E. B. White ended his unforgettable obit (which characteristically was unsigned). "We cannot convey his manner. But with much love in our heart, we say, for everybody, 'All right, Ross. God bless you!' "

# 8

## Don't Miss It If You Can

THE laughter of the Twenties had a sound all its own. I
can hear its echo across the years, belly-deep and uninhibited: the widening grin, the sudden contagious snort, the
rib-splitting guffaws of an entire audience doubled over in a
paroxysm of mirth, holding their sides, slapping their knees
and gasping for breath, the tears streaming down their cheeks.
The sound filled the packed theaters on Broadway where the
great comedians were playing — W. C. Fields and Ed Wynn
and the Marx Brothers and Joe Cook — and the musicians in
the pit would chortle with the audience, and the ushers would
join in the hilarity, and in the deserted lobby the producer
would smile as he counted the profits, because laughter was
what poured golden dollars into the box office.

Those were the days when clowns dressed like clowns, and
wore their motley proudly. The tramp costume, the baggy pants
and absurd headgear, were an integral part of the comic image.
Fields's white cotton gloves and battered top hat (which had a
way of leaping off his head when he was startled, and his pudgy
hands would grab it just in time). Wynn's oversized shoes and
falsetto lisp as he described his latest invention ("It'th an
eleven-foot pole for people I wouldn't touch with a ten-foot

pole.''). Chaplin's jaunty cane and derby. Buster Keaton's pork-pie hat. Bobby Clark's painted spectacles and lecherous leer ("I'm Robert the roué from Reading, P.A."). Fannie Brice's voluminous nightgown in her impersonation of Baby Snooks (*"Daa-*deee!"). Groucho Marx's fierce black mustache, Harpo's blond curls. Joe Cook's ankle-length ulster with its double row of buttons. Dave Chasen's blacked-out tooth and red fright-wig.

When I first saw Joe Cook in 1923, he was co-starring in Earl Carroll's *Vanities* with Peggy Hopkins Joyce, whom he used to refer to as "that somewhat different virgin." I sat in the balcony and marveled at the bland deadpan expression, the slightly curled mouth, the easy flow of nonsense patter as he walked a tightrope or juggled Indian clubs while explaining to the audience why he would not imitate four Hawaiians. (He changed the monologue each night for the private enjoyment of the musicians seated below him.) The climax of the second act was one of those Rube Goldberg contraptions for which Cook was famous, an elaborate machine which occupied the entire stage. At a roll of drums and flourish from the orchestra, Cook yanked a starting lever, wheels turned, pistons rose and fell, gears ground, steam puffed, whistles tooted, and an enormous sledgehammer descended on the red head of Dave Chasen, seated at the far end of the machine and holding a musical triangle. Chasen reacted by striking a single bell-like note on the triangle, and then moved his hand palm-outward in a half-circle before his face, as though to disclaim any credit for his triumph, and grinned.

It was a beatific grin, the perfect foil for Cook's clownery. When a cigar exploded or a hodful of bricks fell, Chasen's face would take on the sheepish expression of one who has just realized that in some way the joke is on him. The head would tilt back, the eyebrows lift like a freight elevator coming up through the sidewalk, the eyes roll upward until the whites showed, and the lips part in a wide smile which revealed the missing center tooth. No matter how often Cook's hammer flattened him, Dave would respond with that same look of wordless wonder, that pleased grin at being noticed, that benign wave of his hand.

Later I saw them together in *Rain or Shine,* and again in *Fine and Dandy,* written by Donald Ogden Stewart, with a program note describing Cook as "a man who would stop at nothing, and frequently does." In this show, as I recall, Cook played the part of a newly hired office manager, inspecting the filing system in a Ross-like attempt to bring a little efficiency into the organization. With grave detachment, he opened a cabinet drawer and took out a very large pair of shoes, which his embarrassed secretary claimed, a striped barber pole, a potted geranium, and finally, showing no particular surprise, a live skunk. (The harassed property man had to keep two skunks backstage, one as an understudy.) Cook was addicted to animals as props. In the subsequent show which Russel Crouse and I wrote for him, he was busy mixing drinks behind the bar when a customer asked for a pousse-café. Unruffled, Joe picked up a cocktail shaker, rattled it a couple of times, removed the lid, and poured out a small and startled cat.

My pleasant, though short-lived, collaboration with Russel Crouse came about through a book he had just published, *It Seems Like Yesterday,* a pictorial history of New York at the turn of the century with photographs of Diamond Jim Brady and Lillian Russell and the old Rector's restaurant. I suggested that the period might provide a nostalgic and colorful atmosphere for a musical comedy. Crouse broached the idea to Joe Cook, who was looking for a new vehicle at the time. Cook was enthusiastic, and we set to work.

I had collaborated once before, with Howard Dietz, on some sketches for *Three's a Crowd,* but that was easy; I turned over a humorous article I had published, Dietz dramatized it, and we split the check. Writing a whole play with someone else was a different matter, and I wondered how two authors could possibly compose at the same typewriter, like a duet on a piano. By trial and error, we worked out a satisfactory arrangement: Crouse would man the machine for an hour while I strode up and down the room, and then I would spell him at the keyboard while he paced, occasionally halting and smacking his forehead with the flat of his hand when an idea struck him. He was an ideal collaborator, patient and quick-witted and an indefatigable worker. His self-discipline was rigid; twenty years before, discovering that he could not handle alcohol, he had sworn off and never touched a drop since, despite his friend Sullivan's occasional pleas to break down and have a drink. "I can always tell that Sully is tight," he would grin, "when he tries to get me off the wagon." Once in Paris he and Alison Smith paused at a sidewalk café, where Alison had a Martini while Crouse resolutely sipped a glass of water. He signaled the *garçon* for a second round. "The lady would like another Martini," he said, "and I'll have a little more of the Seine."

He had a genial and gentle sense of humor, and was universally adored by his associates. After he became a successful producer and co-author with Howard Lindsay of such hits as *Life with Father* and *Arsenic and Old Lace* and *The Sound of Music,* the Kansas City *Star* asked him for "just a page perhaps" listing his accomplishments and titles. Crouse obliged with a letter signed "Secretary to Mr. Crouse":

Russel Crouse is the typical Continental boulevardier-type — handsome, devilishly clever, quick on the bon mot, and a little nuts. He is about two weeks older than St. Augustine, Florida. He flies his own plane, runs the 100-yard dash in 1 hour, 17 minutes, makes all his own clothes, plays the glockenspiel with assorted symphony orchestras, and his pastime is making fudge, a sport that was popular in his youth.

He paints pop art, and is known in avant-garde circles as Pop. He loves operettas, especially telephone operettas. You ask about his titles. I believe he has been knighted because he is called Sir by his two valets, three butlers, and one footman or chiropodist. He lives in New York City on the sunny side of the street, and has a summer villa in Villadelphia.

He is a playwright and some of his better known works are "Hamlet," "Abie's Irish Rose," "East Lynne," "Medea," and "Ladies in a Turkish Bath."

Most of our writing was done at the apartment I shared with Frank Sullivan, who would drop in on us every so often to see how the boys in Cell 2 were doing. Strolling into the room one afternoon to bother the workers, he discovered that we had adjourned for a bite to eat, leaving a half-finished page in the typewriter. Sullivan felt the least he could do for his friends would be to complete the page, and he filled it with so many four-letter obscenities that, if the dialogue were spoken on the stage today, it would be hailed as a masterpiece of realism. By midsummer the weather grew too hot to work in New York, and Crouse and Alison Smith hied to my retreat in Freedom, New Hampshire, which boasted a secluded lake and a stone boathouse in a grove of pines overhanging the water. Alison was enchanted with my sylvan beach. "Oh, look," she gurgled, "the lake comes right up to the shore." Alison lived in a state of sublime confusion. When a passing motorist nearly sideswiped the car in which we were riding, she announced indignantly that she was going to have the careless driver arrested. Crouse pointed out that it would be difficult unless she had his license number. "Oh, but I noticed his number as he drove away," she replied. "It's 5-137-12."

"Better write it down before you forget it," Crouse advised.

"I won't forget it," Alison said confidently. "I have a memory system. 5 is for the five fingers on my hand, and 137 was my room at college, and 12 —" She thought a moment. "— is the Twelve Commandments."

*Hunkydory* was the original name of our opus, but in deference to Cook's superstitious belief in three-word titles we changed it to *Hold Your Horses*. It was a satiric period piece — we did elaborate research to make sure the background was authentic — which sought affectionately to mock the stilted manners and fashions of 1900. The plot (unlike his previous shows, it even had a plot) concerned a cabdriver from Cripple Creek, Colorado (Joe Cook, in coachman's hat and long ulster, driving an elderly nag onto the stage), who lost his directions and arrived in New York in the midst of a political crisis. The Tammany bosses were seeking a scapegoat in the scandal which was about to break, and persuaded Joe to run for Mayor, confident that he would be defeated; but his campaign speeches were so bewildering — well, as it turned out, it didn't matter. The whole plot was thrown out by J. J. Shubert during the out-of-town tryout in Boston.

I had been pleased when Lee and Jake Shubert agreed to produce our play, and could not understand Crouse's notable lack of enthusiasm. To be sure, I had heard stories about the Shuberts — the actor walking down Broadway muttering, "Son of a bitch, son of a bitch," and another actor adding, "And so's his brother Jake" — but my first impression, when I met J.J. in his office, was reassuring. In appearance, I admit, he was somewhat less than impressive. He was squat and dumpy, and sagged at the belly. His short little body was as broad in the buttocks as a ferryboat, but from the waist it tapered rapidly upward toward his narrow hunched shoulders, giving him the general shape of an egg. His white-maned head rode well down on the front slope of the egg, and his face was flat-nosed and

Mongolian. He shuffled a little as he stepped forward from his desk to greet us, his hands in his pockets, his head thrust forward and wagging from side to side, like a mud turtle walking perpendicularly on the end of its shell. He was lavish with solemn assurances that his production of *Hold Your Horses* would do artistic justice to our epic. "I want to do something worth while in the theater, boys," he told us with a catch in his voice, "something I can look back on when I'm dead. Your little play here is a work of art. Such wit! Such spontanuity! Maybe it needs a few touches, but we can do that in rehearsal, so don't worry your heads." J.J., I decided loyally, was much maligned.

Each weekend Crouse and I drove out to Joe Cook's estate at Lake Hopatcong, New Jersey, to go over the dialogue with him and develop comic routines. His domain, aptly known as "Sleepless Hollow," was a masterpiece of contrived bedlam. There was a golf course with the putting green shaped like a funnel, so that the merest dub could not fail to score a hole-in-one. A miniature grand opera house contained nine plush seats and four backstage dressing rooms, each tactfully marked "Number 1." On their arrival, guests were escorted to a subterranean bar called "Kelly's," presided over by one of Joe's remarkable henchmen, Ellis Rowland, in a derby hat and black handlebar mustache. Ellis would pause, while mixing drinks and words, to remark sagely to the guests that necessity was the invention of motherhood, or mention that he ran into his friend Cullough the other day — "you know, Cullough of Clark and McCullough" — or invite another of Cook's henchmen, Dave Clark, to sing a few snatches of a song he had composed on the drop of a spur. (Clark had been a successful songwriter, author of "Here Comes Kelly in His Old High Hat," before he was stricken with paresis, which he claimed to have cured with a dose of salts.) Marc Connelly still cherishes the lyric:

Perhaps you know Mr. Higgins,
That high little English chump.
I don't mean to say he's indignant
But still he is short and he's plump.

  (*Chorus*)
  He's too resisting for me, ha ha,
  He's too resisting for me.
  He said that the scen'ry was painted on seas
  And I was impressed to the top of the trees.

(*Second verse*)
I've met him in most ev'ry city,
Got tired of hearing the words.
He taught me the altaphebetic
And still he has got all his nerves.

  (*Second chorus*)
  He's too consisting for me, ha ha,
  Simple as any can be.
  In spite of concessions
  The world seems possessions.
  He's too insisting for me.

After a couple of highballs, the confused guests would be driven over a couple of miles of circling road to an identical bar called "Schulz's," which stood back-to-back to "Kelly's" and was likewise presided over by Ellis, this time in a blond wig and spectacles. The ceiling was hung with every conceivable object which was smaller than a man's hand; Joe would challenge his visitors to think of any item which had been omitted from his collection. His prize museum piece, resting under a bell glass, was the only baseball *not* autographed by Babe Ruth.

"Sleepless Hollow" was a favorite haunt of Connelly and Benchley and Ross and Ed McNamara, the singing Paterson cop who had taken lessons with Caruso. Highlight of the weekend

was a midnight repast of succulent barbecued spareribs, prepared by Dave Chasen according to his own secret recipe. ("The
whole secret," Dave confided to me once, "is to keep the fire
very low, just embers, and grill the meat slowly.") Smacking
his lips, Ross made an impulsive offer: "Chasen, if you ever
decide to get out of show business and earn an honest living, I'll
stake you to a restaurant." Today Chasen's Beverly Hills restaurant, originally backed by Ross, is the showplace of Hollywood.

Meals at the Cook menage tended to be hazardous. A covered
dish might conceal a dry and desiccated dogbone, the sugar
bowl was apt to disgorge a live mouse, and your trick chair had
a way of buckling or even exploding when you sat down.
Anything could happen at "Sleepless Hollow," and, on the
occasion of Shubert's first and last visit, anything did. J.J.
arrived one snowy Sunday noon in a chauffeur-driven limousine,
accompanied by an unidentified blonde show-girl whom he
prudently left in the car. As he trudged up to the front door, he
was greeted by Dave Clark, clad in a gilt-embroidered major-
domo's uniform which might have graced the Court of St.
James's. Very politely he removed Shubert's fur-collared over-
coat, opened the hall window, and tossed it out into a snow-
drift. Ignoring J.J.'s goggle-eyed look, Clark led the way to the
dining room, where the rest of us were already seated, pulled
out the chair at the head of the table, and sat down in it
himself. Left to his own devices, Shubert wandered dazedly
around the table till he found a vacant seat at the far end. He
had barely started his meal when Clark rapped his glass with a
knife, and rose to speak. It was a fine tribute to the guest of
honor, opening with the statement: "I may be wrong, but I'm
not far from it." Unable to make head or tail of the double talk,
Shubert sank lower in his seat, darting nervous glances right
and left in search of a way to escape. At last Clark wound up

his speech with a dramatic pause and then the climactic line: "Don't miss it if you can." J.J. disappeared shortly afterward.

We saw Shubert now and then during the rehearsal period, but for the most part he preferred to lurk in the background and leave things to his director, R. H. Burnside, a gaunt dyspeptic man whose previous experience had been limited to staging production numbers at the Hippodrome. Only occasionally did J.J. interfere. We had a line of dialogue in which someone accused Cook of being as drunk as a coot, and Joe, glancing down at his ulster, asked, "What's the matter with this coot?" Shubert wanted the line taken out, a good idea but for the wrong reason. "Coots are disgusting," he explained, "they get in your clothes and bite you." Still he impressed me as kind and fatherly, his white head bowed with responsibility. After a particularly enervating rehearsal, he came up to me and rested a paternal hand on my shoulder. "My boy," he said sadly, "the theater isn't a labor of love. It's a labor of drudgery."

*Hold Your Horses* was booked for a week's tryout at the Tremont Theater in Boston, and Crouse and I were housed nearby at the Ritz, handy for any rewriting that might be required. "Not that there could be any big changes at this late date," I assured him confidently; and he gave me a cryptic smile. Heywood Broun came up from New York to be with Connie Madison, later Mrs. Broun, a chorus girl in the show. Ross was also on hand — his friend Ed McNamara was playing the part of Diamond Jim Brady — and other friends and critics from Manhattan converged on Boston to catch the opening. Alison Smith, viewing the familiar faces at a cocktail party Ross gave before the dress rehearsal, murmured happily, "Everybody in the room is here."

The rehearsal that night was slow in starting. Scenery was still being uncrated and set in place, lighting had to be arranged, seamstresses were hastily altering gowns to fit. It was

after ten o'clock when the theater darkened, the hammering
backstage died down, the chatter of wardrobe mistresses and
stagehands and chorus girls ceased, the footlights came on and
went off and came on again, the orchestra concluded its over-
ture, someone yelled, "Ready with them ropes," and the curtain
rose on old Rector's at the turn of the century. The scene
reflected the languorous mood of the period, just as we had
described it: the soft pastel colors, the champagne buckets and
gleam of white napery, the couples pirouetting gracefully to the
soft strains of a "Merry Widow" waltz. "Upstage," we had
written in our script, "Charles Rector moves amongst the tables,
greeting the celebrities of the day such as Diamond Jim Brady,
Lillian Russell, and John L. Sullivan." Even the fact that Lillian
Russell was wearing modern street clothes — there had been
some mix-up about her costume — did not destroy the illusion.
The charm of Old New York was captured for a magic moment.

But only for a moment. A guttural voice rose from the
shadowy depths of the theater, and a dumpy figure hurried past
me down the center aisle. "Wait a minute! Stop it!" J.J.
shouted, waving his short arms. "Let me have the house lights."

He halted in the front of the auditorium, pivoted, and swept
the sparsely filled rows of seats with a baleful eye.

"If there's any people here not connected with this show," he
announced, "I want them to leave the theater and stop talking.
This ain't a picnic, it's a dress rehearsal, and you folks are only
here on suffrage. We're trying to put on a show tomorrow
night, unnerstand?" He fixed his gaze on R. H. Burnside,
hovering uneasily at his elbow, and his eyes narrowed. "From
now on, I'm giving the orders around here. There's only one
captain of this ship, and that's my brother Lee and me."

In the ensuing hollow silence, he rocked on his heels and
glared at the audience. His eyes encountered Crouse and myself,
huddled in sixth-row seats, but he gave no sign of recognition.

"Do you suppose he wants us to leave, too?" I whispered. "After all, this is our play." "Not after tonight," Crouse replied, but did not elaborate. Satisfied that he had cowed the spectators, Shubert returned to the original object of his wrath. With leveled forefinger, he advanced to the orchestra pit, and pointed at the second violinist. "What's the matter with this man?" he demanded of the conductor. "Why wasn't he playing just now?"

Russell Bennett, the tall and dignified composer and arranger of the music, was wielding the baton himself in the exigencies of dress rehearsal. He blinked at Shubert uncertainly. "But his part calls for a twelve-bar rest at this point," he faltered. "There's nothing written for him in the score."

"Then write him something. I pay him a good salary." He scowled at the actors huddled together on the stage, like sheep in a thunderstorm. "What are all you people standing around like statues?" Suddenly he whirled on Burnside, who cringed and retreated a step. "What kind of a lousy opening number do you call this, anyway? Do you think people are going to pay four-forty to see a lot of statues do a waltz?" His lower lip wobbled in self-pity. "Always at the last minute they leave everything up to me, and more besides."

His hands in his pockets and his head wagging, Shubert trudged up the steps and crossed the footlights and waddled onto the stage. "We're gonna start this thing off with a parade of show girls," he said, waving the Junoesque beauties into line. "Like a four-forty show should be." With the patience of a window dresser, he studied each model in turn, placed both hands on her hips, moved her carefully a few inches to the left or right, and nodded with satisfaction. "Now give me that music again." His feet hopping to keep in step, he led the file of buxom blondes across the stage, his arm around the one in the lead. I groaned to Crouse, "He's turning it into another Shubert production."

"What did you expect — *The Miracle?*" Crouse asked. "Let's go out and get some coffee. It's going to be a long night."

It lasted till dawn. Hour after interminable hour, while stagehands slumbered contentedly on their lucrative overtime and R. H. Burnside sat alone at the rear of the theater with his hand over his eyes, J.J. continued to lead his pulchritudinous parade back and forth, trampling the plot underfoot like a herd of Guernseys, churning our carefully planned story into a muddy wallow. He was in his glory, smirking at the girls, humming to himself, even prancing satyr-like in time with the music. "Give me beauty! I want more beauty!" He draped them voluptuously across steps, around tables, along balconies. He walked them in and out of love scenes, he altered plot scenes to make room for them, he chopped other scenes entirely in which they did not appear. Crouse tried manfully to keep up with the changes, drawing pencil lines through page after page of the script in his lap. I wasn't much help; my mind had gone mercifully numb. All I wanted was to curl up somewhere and close my eyes and forget. "I have to think of everything," I could hear J.J. whining. "What we lack around here is a dearth of good ideas."

It was daylight when we staggered back to the Ritz, but there was no chance for sleep. "We've got to make all these cuts and get the script in some kind of shape," Crouse insisted. His voice was vibrant; he seemed to be enjoying the pressure, to relish the thought of an all-night rewrite session. "Have to work fast," he said happily, as he phoned room service for coffee. "Jake's calling a ten o'clock rehearsal."

Somehow I managed to haul myself back to the theater at ten, groggy with weariness, braced for another violent confrontation with Shubert. To my surprise, he was in a benign mood, relaxed and smiling. "Good news, boys," he greeted us. "I got a hit song for the show. It's a cowboy ballad about a little dog."

I echoed dully, "A dog?"

"My brother Lee phoned from New York, he just bought the rights. He's bringing it up with him this afternoon. It's called 'The Last Round-Up.' "

Even Crouse was shaken out of his calm. "But that's been out for a year. Everybody's heard it."

"So maybe they'll remember it then," J.J. said casually, and sang slightly off-key, "Get along, little doggie, get along, little doggie —"

"Little dogie," I corrected. "A dogie is a calf."

J.J. shrugged. "We already got a horse in the show. What's wrong with a calf? It's going to be the opening number, a big production, cowboys and Indians and all."

"In old Rector's?"

"They're shipping the boots and chaps from the warehouse. We'll put it in tomorrow night. All you boys got to do is find some way to cue it."

"Maybe Buffalo Bill might come in and order a steak," I suggested.

"Or we could change the period of the show to 1600," Crouse offered. "There were still Indians around New York then."

"Sure, you can work something like that," Shubert said in relief, and patted our shoulders. "When you've been in show business as long as I have, you'll find there is always a way out of doing everything."

The rest of that week comes back to me in bits and fragments, like snatches of a nightmare I'd sooner forget. Opening night was an agony of toppling scenery and missed cues and a restless audiences who coughed and sneezed and blew their noses in a steady bronchial protest. Each night it grew progressively worse. On Tuesday I noticed J.J. in a conspiratorial huddle with his brother Lee, a taciturn man with a profile like the Indian on the back of a buffalo nickel. The next day a ventriloquist arrived from New York, and was given the only good melody in the show, "If I Love Again," to croon to his dummy, played by Chasen. The Floradora Sextette was thrown out on Thursday to make room for a pair of adagio dancers. By now I would not have been surprised if Shubert had hired a troupe of Japanese tumblers or a trained seal act. The successive scenes had no more relation to each other than the contents of a vaudeville bill. At one time, I heard later, he seriously considered changing the title to *Shubert's Revue.*

We appealed to Joe Cook, the only person with enough influence to restrain Jake and Lee; but actors, I came to learn, have no interest in anything save their own performance. Joe was unconcerned about the changes; his routines had not been tampered with, and the elimination of the plot had given him room to add a few new ones. Instead of worrying about the play, how about writing him some more laughs? Maybe we could cut the scene in the Mayor's office (the climax of the story) and substitute one of his elaborate mechanical contraptions in time for the New York opening. His imagination caught fire. This time a cannon would go off, and Dave Chasen would drop through a trapdoor. We left him talking eagerly over the phone to Shubert.

As we walked out of Cook's dressing room, Crouse took a theater program from his pocket, and pointed to the credits. " 'Taken from a book by Russel Crouse,' " he read aloud. "Shouldn't that be changed to 'Taken as far as possible from a book by Russel Crouse'?"

He was riding out the turbulence as lightly as a cork on a wave. The hectic days and nights, the lack of sleep, the endless slashing and rewriting troubled him not at all; he thrived on it, in fact, and grew more cheerful as he pounded out new comic lines on his portable. I lay inert on the bed, unable to concentrate, thinking of the year's effort and imagination we had invested in the script. Now Shubert was destroying it as wantonly as a baby taking apart a watch with a hammer. If he had pulled out the scenes one by one over the long rehearsal period, like a dentist extracting a tooth at a time, it might have been easier to adjust myself to the pain; but this sudden demolition of our play, on the eve of its New York opening, was too much to bear.

The bedroom was swimming around me, my head throbbed, and all I could hear was Shubert's whine in my ears: "More life! More spontanuity." I bolted from the room, went down to the lobby, and walked blindly in circles, my fists clenched to keep from yelling aloud. I think that if I had encountered J.J. at that moment, I would have flattened him as effectively as Joe Cook's sledgehammer. Dave Chasen happened to spot me, and put an arm around me and led me to his own room and poured me a tumbler of Scotch. He was the first person who had shown sympathy, and I began to laugh hysterically and wound up sobbing on his shoulder. I suppose he saw that I was on the verge of cracking up, and he suggested quietly that I take a train to New Hampshire and spend a day or so at my Freedom home until I got hold of myself. His understanding was the only thing that saved me from going completely to pieces. Whatever else the Cook show accomplished, it earned me a lifelong friend in Dave.

Crouse never quite forgave me for running out on him. When I returned to Boston on Saturday, just in time for the end of the engagement, his greeting was cordial enough; but it was clear, I could see, that any prospect of further collaboration was ended. He was devoted to the theater, his energy was prodigious, and he had no tolerance for defection or weakness in a partner. I didn't blame him; I felt the same way myself. I could not go through such an ordeal again, and I resolved then and there that I would never attempt another play. The theater, as J.J. said, was a labor of drudgery.

*Hold Your Horses* opened at the Winter Garden to mingled reviews. Gilbert Gabriel wrote sadly that the basic story had charm and appeal, but Shubert had loaded its pockets with so many gadgets and geegaws that it had stretched and sagged out of shape until it dragged along the ground. Somehow, to my surprise and Shubert's self-satisfaction, the show caught on and ran for over half a year; but I never went back to see it after opening night. An agent on the West Coast wired that David Selznick wanted to sign me for a stint at RKO Studios. Could I come at once?

Hollywood, like Broadway, had found that laughter was a rich bonanza. Full-length features by Chaplin and Keaton and Lloyd were box-office successes, comedy was in mounting demand, and with the advent of sound, film companies were raiding the East for humor writers. Benchley was on his way west to work at RKO. Mrs. Parker and Donald Ogden Stewart were already on the Coast. Frank Sullivan, who had a phobia about travel, received a five-hundred-word telegram from a Hollywood producer, offering to make all arrangements, from a drawing room on the Super Chief to enough sodium amytal for the trip. Sullivan's reply was brief: DON'T BE SILLY.

I was not so wise. My overpowering urge to be a continent's width away from J.J. may have decided me. I wired acceptance; and so I quit the frying pan for the fire.

# 9

## Go West Yourself, Mr. Greeley

DAVID SELZNICK was president of RKO Studios, at the time of my first Hollywood assignment, and his older brother Myron Selznick was my West Coast agent. Myron was easygoing and jolly — "Go out and earn that 90 percent commission I pay you," he liked to tell his clients — and immensely crafty. It was his ingenious scheme to sell me to Dave under two separate contracts, one in my own name and one in the name of John Riddell. I lacked the nerve to go through with it; though, looking back now, I suspect I was being overcautious. The odds were that my dual role would never have been detected, in that wild and woolly confusion which was Hollywood at the beginning of the Thirties.

Writers at RKO were housed in a long one-story stucco building, each cubicle identical, like the rooms in a cheap motel. The windows faced on a courtyard of parched grass, bordered with big bilious flowers which, as Don Marquis had written me, were odorless and looked as if they had been cut out of paper. My office was equipped with a telephone (no outside calls), a typewriter (which never worked), and a leather swivel chair (obviously a mistake, because after two days it was replaced by a wooden one). I had heard how Hollywood writers were chained to their desks and fed on pans of gruel shoved through the bars of their cells; but RKO gave us considerable freedom. We were allowed to speak to each other as we passed in the corridor, take our daily exercise in the yard without supervision by guards, and eat at noon in the same commissary with the producers and directors and actors, although at an isolated table in the rear. The rest of our day was spent reading the *Hollywood Reporter* and waiting for a summons from the front office.

One of my fellow inmates was William Faulkner, whose cell was three doors from mine. With a misuse of talent which approached sheer lunacy, the studio had assigned this earthy chronicler of Yoknapatawpha County to write a sophisticated drama of New York society, a background about which he knew nothing and cared less. After staring blankly at the bare walls of his office for several days, he smuggled a message to Dave Selznick, asking if he might be permitted to work at home instead of coming to the office every day. A couple of weeks later, Selznick decided to confer with him about the progress of the script and phoned his hotel, to be informed that Faulkner had checked out some time previously. A search of all the lodging places in the Los Angeles area failed to disclose any trace. At last a frantic long-distance call located him back in Oxford, Mississippi. Home, to Bill, was where he could take his shoes off.

Hollywood seemed to have no conception of what to do with the writers it imported from the East. My assignment was a vehicle for Joel McCrea called *Sports Page,* a grim exposé of the professional wrestling racket, totally bereft of comedy. Just as illogically, Robert Benchley had been given the task of dramatizing the newspaper strip *Little Orphan Annie,* which fortunately was never produced. His cell at RKO was at the far end

of the writers' block, and each morning we would exchange
greetings as he passed my window on his tardy way to work.
One morning he showed up suffering from what I could see was
the grandfather of all hangovers, his hands shaky, his face a
ghastly gray. I asked solicitously if he'd had breakfast. *"Had
it?"* he shuddered. "I've thrown it up." A garden hose was
lying on the grass, parallel to the walk; and as Benchley made
his way painfully toward his office, the gardener gave it an
absent-minded flip, sending a snakelike ripple down its length
past him. Benchley cast one horrified look, turned on his heel,
and drove back to the Garden of Allah and went to bed.

A number of Eastern expatriates stayed at the Garden of
Allah, a rococo arrangement of bungalows and winding paths
and palm trees, because it was conveniently located on Sunset
Boulevard near the studio, or at least as near as anything is to
anything else in Hollywood. It was said to have been named for
Alla Nazimova, the silent screen star, who had built it as a real
estate investment at the peak of her success. Benchley shared a
bungalow with Charles Butterworth, a deft comedian whose
sharp-profiled face was cast in a permanent expression of
gloom. In one of his Broadway musicals, someone tried to cheer
him up by reminding him that it was spring. "Spring!" Butterworth said morosely. "Spring air rots things." He picked up a
teacup and shattered it against the wall. "See? All rotten."
Butterworth, like Benchley, had a particular aversion to the
songbirds which abounded in the shrubbery around the cottages
and shrilled incessantly while he was trying to sleep. Returning
from a party in the darkness before dawn, he roamed the
grounds in a mood of dire revenge, shaking the palm trees one
after another to disturb any roosting occupants. "Wake me up,
would you, you feathered bastards?" I could hear him muttering
outside my window. "All right, now it's *my* turn."

While living at the Garden of Allah that summer, Benchley

came down with a slight case of pneumonia, and called in a doctor who was badly afflicted with first person pluralism, or we disease. (This is a common ailment in the medical profession; in a similar way, the prizefight manager instructs his man to get in there and slug, he can't hurt us.) Bright and early each morning the doctor would stride into his bedroom and inquire in a booming voice, "Well, well, well, and how do we feel this morning?" Benchley stood it as long as he could, but it became clear that something had to be done. That night he and Butterworth ripped open a sofa pillow, and Butterworth smeared some glue on Benchley's posterior and pasted it with feathers. The following morning, when the doctor asked, "How do we feel?", Benchley sighed, "We don't think we're doing so well, doc," and rolled over onto his stomach and yanked down the bedcovers. He was up and around that same afternoon, but the doctor didn't recover for a week.

Benchley was the first of us to finish his stretch at RKO and head for New York in relief. As he departed from the Garden of Allah, after distributing gratuities right and left to the staff, a doorman approached him and held out an upturned palm. Inasmuch as Benchley had never seen the man before, his Yankee blood rebelled against being imposed on for another tip. He started to brush past, but the doorman asked pointedly, "Aren't you going to remember me, sir?" "Why, of course," Benchley said with a bright smile as he climbed into a taxi, "I'll write you every day."

In those early Thirties the studios were still going through a period of scrambling readjustment. The industry (as Hollywood liked to call itself) had not yet recovered from its shock in the fall of 1927 when Warner Brothers, having gambled everything on a device called Vitaphone, released the first talking picture. *The Jazz Singer,* starring Al Jolson, earned a couple of million dollars and triggered the revolution. For a time the other companies tried to hold out against sound — it would cost a fortune to build new stages, install expensive equipment, wire all their theaters across the country — but public demand made the changeover inevitable. By the end of the decade, even the most stubborn executive had realized that silence was no longer golden. When Greta Garbo made her talking debut in 1930 in *Anna Christie* (GARBO TALKS!, M-G-M's billboards screamed) her opening line, "Gif me a viskey, ginger ale on the side — und don't be stingy, baby," signaled the end of an era. Charlie Chaplin was the longest hold-out, releasing his soundless *City Lights* in 1931, and another silent, *Modern Times,* as late is 1936; but other stars of the sub-title days hastened to take voice lessons and modify their sweeping melodramatic gestures. Some of them could not adapt themselves to the new medium and faded into obscurity: John Gilbert, the great lover of the screen, whose high squeaky tenor made audiences titter; Emil Jannings, who received the Academy Award in 1928 and returned to Germany that same year, unable to overcome his thick guttural accent; Clara Bow, the girl who had "It" but nothing else; Norma Talmadge, Corinne Griffith, Billie Dove. In his novel of Hollywood, *The Last Tycoon,* Scott Fitzgerald quoted one of these plaintive victims of progress: "I had a beautiful place in 1928. All spring I was up to my ass in daisies."

Comedy underwent the same drastic change. During the silent era, custard-pie routines and Keystone Cops chases dominated Hollywood's comic thinking, and the transition to more sophisticated entertainment was slow and painful. To be sure, there had been flashes of authentic humor in the Twenties. Buster Keaton was brilliantly funny in 1922 in *Day Dreams,* forerunner of "The Secret Life of Walter Mitty," in which he portrayed among other roles a henpecked caveman whose outsize wife carried the club, and a Christian martyr thrown to a very bored lion. Keaton's chiseled profile, as classic as Barrymore's, never changed expression, and his wide eyes looked out gravely on a hostile world; he was, to my thinking, an even more inspired pantomimist than Charlie Chaplin. Chaplin's most productive period was before the Twenties, but *The Gold Rush* (1925), with his portrayal of the starving prospector cooking his boot and delicately winding the laces onto his fork like strands of spaghetti, was a moment of genuine comic genius. There were other silent masterpieces: Harold Lloyd's *Safety Last* (1923) and *The Freshman* (1925); Laurel and Hardy in *Leave 'em Laughing* (1928); and Raymond Griffith's Civil War spy parody called *Hands Up,* which contained one surprise twist which I have never seen topped.

It seemed that Griffith, a Northern secret agent in a silk hat and opera cape, had been captured and placed against a wall before a Confederate firing squad. This was no ordinary firing squad; it was composed of crack marksmen, the very cream of Kentucky's expert skeet-shooters. A hopeless situation, it appeared; but Griffith, with perfect aplomb, snatched a plate from a girl's picnic basket, secreted it in his cape, and at the command "Fire!" scaled it aloft. Automatically every rifle lifted to hit the flying target, while Griffith vaulted the wall and was gone. The advent of talkies ended his career. Griffith suffered from a throat malignancy, and could not raise his voice above a hoarse whisper. His last screen appearance — and I can see his face now when I shut my eyes — was in 1930 in *All Quiet on the Western Front.* Griffith was the stubble-bearded French poilu who leaped into a shellhole and was bayoneted by the young German, played by Lew Ayres, and lay inert during the rest of the scene, his open eyes staring and his features fixed in an unforgettable mask of death.

Zasu Pitts was another casualty of sound. A distinguished dramatic actress whose delicate beauty was reminiscent of

Lillian Gish, she had achieved stardom early in the Twenties as the tragic heroine of Eric Von Stroheim's *Greed;* but after that she had been relegated to playing comic bits as a scatterbrained spinster. Her chance to reestablish herself as a tragedian came when Lewis Milestone cast her as Lew Ayres's ailing mother in *All Quiet.* She gave the finest performance of her career; but the preview audience recognized her and broke into such peals of laughter that the whole scene had to be scrapped and reshot with Beryl Mercer as the conventional screen mother. Miss Pitts never attempted another dramatic role.

Inevitably writers were the last to be accepted into the new order. In the days before sound, a star comedian made up his story as he went along, aided by a swarm of anonymous gagmen who could be had for a dime a dozen. Directors needed no dialogue, and writers commanded little salary and less respect. The attitude was hard to overcome. Long after talkies arrived, the *Hollywood Reporter* held strictly to its policy of never, never including an author's name in the list of screen credits. The only exception was when Douglas Fairbanks and Mary Pickford made their first talking picture in 1929, *The Taming of the Shrew,* and a reluctant small-print acknowledgment read: "Play by William Shakespeare, with additional dialogue by Director Samuel Taylor."

I left RKO at the drop of an option, thoroughly disillusioned and resolved, like everyone else from the East, that I would never return; and, like everyone else, I came back to Hollywood a few years later. I was on my way home from Alaska, after a summer with the Eskimos along the Bering Sea, when a cable reached me in Juneau, asking me to report immediately to the Hal Roach Studio to work on a "Topper" picture starring Roland Young. Southern California was in the midst of a September heat wave when I arrived, attired in heavy woolens which had felt quite comfortable amid the Arctic ice floes. My suit was saturated with perspiration before the airport taxi reached town, and all I wanted, as Mr. Benchley was credited with saying, was to get out of my wet clothes and into a dry Martini.

Hollywood had come of age since my last visit. The industry had finally mastered the technique of sound, desegregation of writers was under way, and its own Golden Decade of Humor had dawned. New comic talents were emerging from the ranks to bolster those old standbys, Keaton and Chaplin and Lloyd. Zasu Pitts, with her helpless fluttering hands and quaking voice, displayed a blend of drollery and pathos which in my opinion exceeded Chaplin's. Marie Dressler had graduated from the broad slapstick of *Tillie's Punctured Romance* to reveal herself, in *Tugboat Annie,* as a comedienne of rare poignancy and power. Wallace Beery, a burly heavy of the silent films, developed into the fine and sensitive artist of *The Champ.* Laurel and Hardy forsook pie-throwing to pose as Christmas tree salesmen in *Big Business,* possibly the most hilarious short ever produced, directed with flawless timing by Leo McCarey. Former glamour stars were showing unexpected ability in light farce. The exotic Carole Lombard proved to be one of the screen's nimblest clowns in *My Man Godfrey.* Myrna Loy had been typed as an Oriental seductress and William Powell had played a smooth society con man before they teamed up in the sophisticated and witty "Thin Man" series. Claudette Colbert and Clark Gable won Academy Awards for their expert comedy in Frank Capra's *It Happened One Night.*

Most of Broadway's famous funnymen trickled west during the Thirties to swell the mounting flood of humor: Ed Wynn in *Manhattan Mary;* the four Marx Brothers in *Animal Crackers,* with Margaret Dumont as the durable victim of their mayhem; Charles Ruggles and Roland Young and Charles Laughton in

*Ruggles of Red Gap.* And, in the middle of the decade, W. C. Fields's immortal characterization of Micawber in *David Copperfield,* matched only by Roland Young's perfect portrayal of the unctuous Uriah Heep.

Roland Young was the very pattern of a gentleman, slight of build, erect and poised, with an aristocratic beaked nose and a long upper lip which terminated in a pencil-mustache, as carefully clipped as his enunciation. His mouth barely moved when he spoke — Bill Fields used to call him "Stingy Lips" — and his voice had a way of breaking off in a plaintive little whimper. He was the Broadway star of Shaw's *The Devil's Disciple* and *Beggar on Horseback* by Kaufman and Connelly, a talented artist whose sketches had appeared in *Life* and *Vanity Fair,* and a raconteur and sly wit. (When I asked him what ever became of Freddie Bartholomew, who had the name role in *David Copperfield,* Roland said thinly, "Basil Rathbone ate him.") In *Topper,* based on Thorne Smith's fantasy, he played the part of a staid and proper banker, henpecked by Mrs. Topper (Billie Burke) and haunted by a pair of well-meaning ghosts (Cary Grant and Constance Bennett). A superb actor, he could convey the impression of being whisked around a dance floor by a disembodied spirit, or propelled helplessly down a corridor with his arms held by his two spectral companions. When the invisible Constance Bennett tickled him or mussed his hair — a fine bit of trick photography — he would giggle idiotically, and then try to explain his strange conduct to the bewildered onlookers. Sometimes Miss Bennett would materialize unexpectedly in his bedroom, and Roland's mobile features would register sheer anguish as he sought to conceal her presence from his wife.

The first "Topper" picture was so successful that the studio decided to make a sequel, *Topper Takes a Trip,* which was already in production when I arrived on the Hal Roach lot.

Roland Young, Corey Ford, and director Norman McLeod on the
set of *Topper Takes a Trip*.

Since my duty was to supply additional dialogue, I had to follow it from set to set, inventing new lines during the shooting or writing all night to prepare a scene for tomorrow's schedule. This meant working at the elbow of the director, Norman Z. McLeod, whose nimble mind and fey sense of humor were ideally fitted to an antic ghost story. Norm had worked his way up from a gagman in the early Mack Sennett days to become one of Hollywood's leading directors — *Alice in Wonderland, The Secret Life of Walter Mitty* with Danny Kaye, and a number of the Crosby-Hope "Road to" series. He was tall and solidly built, a former light heavyweight champion at the University of Washington, but his bearing was deceptively gentle, and his voice was pitched so low that sometimes I had to bend forward to hear him. "I'm as quiet as a mouse peeing on a blotter," he confessed sheepishly. His subdued manner infected the set until everyone moved on tiptoes and even the carpenters and grips talked in hushed tones as they worked. Once during a lunch break the phone rang on the deserted stage, and a solitary watchman lifted the receiver and breathed "Hello" in a sepulchral whisper.

My second sojourn on the Coast turned out to be as pleasant as my first had been frustrating. The Hal Roach Studio was intimate and charming, attractively laid out with private cottages like an exclusive summer resort, and small enough so that everyone knew everyone else and worked together as one contented family (except Miss Bennett, who remained aloof and coldly superior). Hal Roach had given a free hand to his talented young executive producer, Milton Bren, a happy extrovert who loved to tell self-deprecating stories about his early days in Los Angeles as a Jewish tailor's son. There was the time that Dad Bren strolled onto a waterfront pier where a crowd had gathered, and craned his neck in vain to see the source of all the excitement. At last the crowd dispersed, and he gazed at an enormous fish lying on the planks. " 'I asked the man what it was,' " Milt quoted his father, " 'and he said it was a Jewfish. So I walked away; I didn't want to make any trouble.' "

Milt was a natural clown and excellent mimic. One afternoon we were on location, filming a barnyard scene with pigs and geese and chickens. While the equipment was being set up, Milt and Norm McLeod and I took refuge from the sun in the tent of Billie Burke, a sweet-faced and wonderfully funny lady. A hen was making strident noises outside, and Milt did an impromptu imitation which we applauded. Pleased by his success, he challenged Miss Burke: "Billie, can you go like a chicken?" "Not any more," Miss Burke replied with a wistful sigh.

To keep ahead of the shooting schedule, Norm and I would work on the script evenings and weekends at his Toluca Lake home in North Hollywood; and so it was that I met his wife, former socialite Evelyn Ward, known to one and all as Bunny. There has never been anyone else like Bunny; they broke the mold after she was cast. She was diminutive and cute as an Easter rabbit, with a button nose that wrinkled when she laughed. Her hair was done up in a bun and, to carry out her nickname still further, she usually wore a cloche hat with two bunny ears. Even her mind was like a rabbit, running in circles, doubling back on its tracks, darting off at an unexpected angle to throw the listener off the trail. "I'm a split personality all in one," she informed me happily. Bunny was aware of her tendency to turn ideas inside out. "But you can't blame me for making a mistake now and then," she insisted. "After all, nobody's human." Then, to clear it all up, she added, "I must have had my mind on something I was thinking about."

Her inverted sentences, which Norm called Bunnyisms, constituted a sort of mental skid. It was more than a slip of the tongue; it was a slip of the whole mind, a blurred double exposure in which one thought was printed on top of another. "For your information," Bunny would say, "let me ask you a question." Or, to an engaged couple, "Two can live as cheaply as one, but it costs them twice as much." Or the night we were watching the fights at Jeffries' Barn, and she took a dislike to one of the contenders. "He's muscle-drunk," she announced. I asked her if she was referring to the boxer in the black trunks. "No," she said, "I mean that other-looking fellow."

Skid-talk is like a time bomb; it ticks away in your sub-conscious and suddenly, a few minutes later, your mind explodes with the realization that something about the remark you just heard was slightly askew. After dining with friends one evening, Bunny complimented the hostess, "Darling, that was the best salad I ever put in my whole mouth." She was very enthusiastic about the picture Norm and I were working on. "I hope it goes over with a crash," she said loyally. Her insults were equally bewildering. Once she told Constance Bennett very candidly, "I never liked you, and I always will." And I suspect a perennially young starlet is still trying to decipher Bunny's crusher: "You're old enough to be my daughter."

The insidious thing about what she said was that it sounded perfectly sane as she said it. When a party she was giving at the Toluca Lake residence became so boisterous that it threatened to disturb the neighbors, Bunny warned the merrymakers, "Remember, this isn't the only house you're in." Staying one night at a hotel, she phoned room service: "Send me up some hot water juice and a lemon." Again, having rescued a fledgling robin which had fallen out of a tree, she explained to me, "I believe in being dumb to kind animals." I became an avid collector of Bunnyisms, jotting down such prime examples of mental slippage as:

"You can't make a sow's purse out of a cow's ear."

"From time immoral."

"It was so dark you couldn't see your face in front of you."

"Norman tells me a thing one day and out the other."

"I'm laughing with my head off."

Bunny was the best skid-talker I've ever known, but J. J. Shubert ran her a close second. (When I described my troubles with the Shuberts, Bunny shrugged: "Too many cooks in the soup.") Samuel Goldwyn was another serious contender for first honors with his ability to garble the language: "What a day to spend Sunday," for example, or his introduction of Jackie Coogan's mother as "the goose that laid the golden egg," or his remark when he presented Danny Kaye with a generous bonus on the birth of a baby girl: "Here's a little bird's nest for your daughter." And surely some special award should go to President Lyndon Johnson. I lay awake half the night trying to untangle a statement he made during the election campaign: "For the first time in history, profits are higher than ever before." But my favorite will always be Bunny's affectionate message to me after I left for the East: "We miss you as much as if you were here."

From time to time, during the shooting of *Topper Takes a Trip*, Norm McLeod and Roland Young and I would leave the studio at noon for a leisurely lunch hour or two at Mr. Benchley's apartment. Frequently we were joined by Scott Fitzgerald, who was working next door at M-G-M and who would wait for us in his battered car outside the Hal Roach gate. (He'd had a feud with Roach, and was barred from the lot.) The Benchley apartment was small and had only one entrance, and delivery boys were forever elbowing guests aside as they crossed the living room on their way to the kitchen. The most prominent furnishing was a bar made of two upended cartons, well stocked, and promptly on our arrival Benchley would busy himself mixing drinks. Scott Fitzgerald, who had recently gone on the wagon, shook his head in mock disapproval. "Don't you know that drinking is slow death?" "So who's in a hurry?" Benchley asked, stirring a Martini contentedly.

If a man can properly be described as beautiful, Fitzgerald was just that: a sensitive mouth, deep dreaming eyes, features as fragile as porcelain. I have never known anyone more dedicated to his profession. He would whip out a pad from his pocket and make notes as I talked, a highly flattering procedure until he explained, "I just thought of a phrase I didn't want to forget. Now, then, what were you saying?" His mind never ceased working, inventing, creating, and that was probably what made him the supreme craftsman he was. (Jim Thurber, I was pleased to learn during a conversation, felt as I did that *The Great Gatsby* was the finest novel of our generation, and would be remembered long after the current critical furor over Hemingway had died out.) In all the welter of biographies and warped fictional portraits like *The Disenchanted* which have been published since Scott's death, no one has brought out the basic fact that he was a poet, who possessed the priceless gift of working magic with words, of transforming the ordinary into something shining and precious. "The moon soaked with wet light his tangled clothes on the floor." "We drove over to Fifth Avenue, warm and soft, almost pastoral on the summer Sunday afternoon. I wouldn't have been surprised to see a great flock of white sheep turn the corner." (I've never seen Fifth Avenue since without looking for the sheep.) Or the haunting last line of *Gatsby:* "So we beat on, boats against the current, borne back ceaselessly into the past."

Scott was hard at work on *The Last Tycoon,* his final book, but on evenings when he could break away he would meet me at my hotel and we would dine together at Dave Chasen's restaurant. I was living then at the Château Marmont on Sunset Strip, in a rear top-floor apartment with a private balcony. I seldom stepped out on it; there was nothing to see but a bare hillside where bulldozers were gouging out new building sites, one drab excavation below another. Sandy rubble had spilled down from the successive terraces, and was grown over with coarse trailing weeds. One night Scott arrived early; and while I was pouring myself a highball (he was not drinking) he wandered out onto the balcony. I joined him, prepared to apologize for the view, but his face was radiant. He pointed to the vine-covered terraces, bathed in moonlight. "The hanging gardens of Babylon," he said; and from then on my view was enchanted, and I could not wait to get home each night to look at it again. That, I submit, is the definition of a writer.

Chasen's was my favorite eating place, because Dave was my bosom friend, because his food was the finest in town, and because everyone else I knew liked to eat there too. Dave was a peripatetic host, darting around the restaurant in quick erratic passage, worried, solicitous, never still. All evening long he would skip from table to table, hovering at the elbow of a guest to suggest tonight's special — *boeuf aux champignons,* perhaps, or lobster flown direct from Maine — or pausing in midflight to exchange a quick story with Jimmy Stewart, or argue a golf score with Grantland Rice, or stoop over with elaborate pantomime to part the feathers of Hedda Hopper's hat and remove a hen's egg he had palmed. Whenever he spotted an acquaintance from Broadway, his eyes would light and he would pass a hand palm-outward before his face in that mute gesture for which he was famous.

Today his establishment is Hollywood's leading *bistro,* the swank gathering place of film celebrities, constantly sprouting new wings to accommodate Dave's ever growing clientele; but success was a long time coming. Joe Cook's health had failed after *Hold Your Horses,* his last Broadway appearance, and a creeping paralysis had ended his juggling days; and Dave had headed west to seek work in pictures. His reputation as an amateur chef had preceded him across the continent, and between screen tests he used to visit the homes of friends and obligingly put on barbecue spreads. Frank Capra pointed out that if he were going to spend his time slaving over a hot grill, he might as well get paid for it; and Dave thought of Harold Ross's offer to put up the money if he ever decided to go into the restaurant business. He wrote a letter east, and Ross wired the necessary three thousand dollars. (The eventual return from his investments in Chasen's came to something over $200,000, a fact which worried Ross. "Goddam it, I never intended to make money out of Dave's place," he told Thurber guiltily.) Dave opened a spareribs and chili parlor on Beverly Boulevard, named it for no good reason the Southern Pit Barbecue, and stood back to await the stampede of customers.

They stampeded very slowly at first, and business was so poor that Dave had to shanghai people he knew and drive them to his restaurant. Once there, he found it just as hard to drive them away. They would turn a deaf ear to his pleas that it was time to go home, and on one occasion, when he threatened to turn out the lights, Joel Sayre picked him up bodily, tossed him outside and locked the door, and the customers returned to their all-night poker game.

The Southern Pit Barbecue, Sayre recalls, was a tiny single-story stucco building with six tables, an eight-stool counter, a six-stool bar, and a single stove in the closet-size kitchen. Dave did all the cooking, most of the serving, helped with the dishwashing, worked behind the bar, and took care of the marketing — not a great task, since he offered only two dishes, chili at a quarter a bowl, and barbecued spareribs at thirty-five cents a pair. Today Chasen's menu lists over 150 items, he averages five hundred meals in the course of an evening, and customers awaiting tables line the bar three or four deep.

An air of informality has marked the restaurant from its very outset. W. C. Fields and Gregory La Cava used to indulge in endless profane games of Ping-Pong in the garden behind the restaurant, coached by Spencer Tracy. Groucho Marx or Jimmy Durante might go into a comic routine at any moment. Jimmy Cagney and Ed McNamara and Pat O'Brien and Frank McHugh would lift their voices in Hibernian harmonies in a corner. Dave kept his choicest liquors locked in the office safe, but Humphrey Bogart and Peter Lorre managed to lug safe and contents out into the street and almost had it in a cab before they were apprehended. When Charles Butterworth left his brand-new sports car parked outside, friends took down the front doors of the restaurant and drove it into the dining room. Dave likes to recall the night that Robert Benchley made his way to the street, slightly tiddly, and signaled to a uniformed man at the curb: "Call me a taxi." The man drew himself up with great dignity and replied, "Sir, I happen to be a rear admiral in the United States Navy."

"All right, then," Benchley said affably, "call me a battle-ship."

Visitors from the East — Alexander Woollcott and Nunnally Johnson and James Thurber and, of course, Harold Ross — would make Chasen's their headquarters during a Hollywood stay; though Ross never liked Hollywood, and felt that writers who deserted his magazine to work in pictures were nothing less than traitors. When a Los Angeles newspaper asked him to comment on former staff members who had made important contributions to the film industry, Ross sat down at Chasen's typewriter and hammered out a blistering statement that not a single writer worth his salt had ever left *The New Yorker* for Hollywood.

One evening at Chasen's, Thurber disappeared into the men's room for several hours, and decorated every inch of wall space

Dave Chasen, Nunnally Johnson, and Harold Ross at
Chasen's Restaurant. (Courtesy of Dave Chasen.)

with an elaborate mural depicting the Battle of the Sexes. Dave's delight at this priceless adornment was short-lived. The following morning he was met at the men's room door by a cleaning woman, weary but triumphant. "Some drunk scribbled all over the walls in there," she told her stricken employer, "but I finally got it washed off."

There are times, Dave admits today, when he longs for the old Joe Cook days, sledgehammer and all. "Joe's hammer never gave me a headache like the restaurant business," he sighs. If a half-dozen important customers arrive simultaneously, and all demand to be seated at once, Dave has to soothe their feelings by buying them drinks at the bar, or rushing a platter of hors-d'oeuvres from the kitchen to keep them happy until a booth is ready. Drunks must be eased out tactfully without offending them, temperamental stars mollified if they are not seated in the best light, table-hoppers discouraged, autograph-seekers and photographers barred. Only the devoted care of his lovely wife Maude has kept him from cracking under the nightly strain.

The sole place he can light a pipe and relax is in his little office at the rear of the restaurant, hung with photographs and mementoes which go back over a lifetime in show business. Here in this quiet sanctum sanctorum his intimate friends have traditionally gathered each night before dinner to banter laughs with Dave; and here I have spent some of my most cherished Hollywood moments in the company of Charles Laughton and Elsa Lanchester, Jack Dempsey, Fred McMurray, Frank Capra, Eddie Sutherland, Red Skelton, Leo McCarey, Bing Crosby, Ben Hecht, Gene Fowler, Billy Grady, W. C. Fields, or other members of Dave's inner circle. Many of them are gone now, summoned by what Fields used to call the Man in the Bright Nightgown, but the room still echoes to their remembered laughter.

It was at Chasen's — or, rather, on the sidewalk in front of it — that I first encountered W. C. Fields in person. As I was about to enter the restaurant, I noticed a vaguely familiar figure, his back turned toward me, listening with grave attention to an impoverished actor who was putting the bite on him for a handout. And then I heard that unmistakable foghorn of a voice, sanctimonious and blatantly fraudulent. "I'm sorry, my good man," Fields explained sadly, "but all my money is tied up in currency." And, with a courtly bow, the Great Man strode inside.

# 10

## *The One and Only*

W. C. FIELDS is generally acknowledged to be the supreme comic artist of his time, in my own opinion the funniest man who ever lived, and he was even funnier offstage than on. His drawn-out rasping voice was the same, of course, but he had an infectious giggle, a falsetto he-he-he-he-he like the chirp of a cricket, which I never heard him use in his professional work. His everyday speech was extravagantly florid. "Methinks," he would intone, "there's a Nubian in the fuel supply." Due to his zealous reading of the eighteenth-century English romanticists, their stilted phraseology came naturally to his lips — "Betwixt" or "Forsooth" or "Hither and yon" — and he was the only person I've known to start a sentence with the word "Likely."

That occurred one night when Fields and I were having dinner at Chasen's. We were in one of the semicircular booths along the wall, and Bill by preference was facing the rear of the restaurant. Over his shoulder I could see Sabu, the Elephant Boy, making one of his elaborate entrances, clad in Indian robes and followed by two tall Sikh bearers (probably from Central Casting) with white turbans wound on their heads. The *chokras* stood with arms folded while Sabu seated himself in the booth next to ours, back to back with Fields. Bill had become conscious of the commotion behind him, and he swung his head slowly around, his gaze moving like the beam of a revolving harbor light until it fixed on Sabu with a baleful glare. Out of the corner of his mouth, in an aside which could have been heard clear to Santa Barbara, he growled to me, "Likely the little mahout will mistake my nose for a proboscis, and climb on my sho-o-oulder."

We had a weekly date to dine together at Chasen's, joined sometimes by Roland ("Stingy Lips") Young or Billy Grady, Fields's former business manager and vituperative companion, or Dave himself when he had a free moment. Over his eighth or ninth Martini, Bill was wont to lapse into sentimental recollections of his experiences in show business. "Got the theater in my blo-o-od," he would drawl. "My great uncle Fortescue used to be a Swiss bell-ringer at Elks' smokers. Ah, yaas, poor old Uncle Fortescue. Run over by a horse-car in Scollay Square, Boston, after attending a musi-*cale* at the Parker House." I never knew how much of what he said was factual, for Fields, a true artist, constantly embellished his stories with new imaginative touches. It didn't matter. Bill could have recited the alphabet and had me rolling on the floor.

He had toured the world, under the auspices of Tex Rickard, and loved to boast of his travels to Samoa and Australia. "Once I fell in love with a Melanesian belle," he would reminisce, "a charming little savage with kinky hair that bristled like a barberry hedge. A *bar-r-rb'*ry hedge, yaas. Had a wooden soup dish in her nether lip, and through her nose was a brass ring from a missionary's hitching post. Prettiest gal on the island." Or: "One day in Melbourne whilst strolling down the street I observed a number of vehicles drawn up before a sumptuous mansion. So I went up to the door, and a butler stuck a silver plate under my nose. I contributed an old laundry slip and a dime, and went in. Most enjoyable soiree, most enjoyable. I had a long talk with the governor's wife."

"What did you talk about?" I asked.

"We discussed the mating habits of the wallaby."

Now and then he would dwell on his early boyhood in Germantown, a suburb of Philadelphia. He was born William Claude Dukenfield, the son of poor but dishonest parents. His mother would lie abed until midday — "besotted with gin," Bill emphasized to me carefully — and when she heard the noon whistle she would leap to her feet, pausing only to tie on an apron and dash some water over her face. Then she would stand on the front steps, mopping the bogus perspiration from her brow with a corner of the apron, and sighing, "Been working all morning over a hot stove" as the neighbors walked by. "Good day to ye, Mrs. Muldoon," she would beam, and add, after the stroller was out of hearing, "Terrible gossip, Mrs. Muldoon. Oh, and how are *you* today, Mrs. Frankel?" Another pause as she passed. "Nasty old bitch, Mrs. Frankel. Ah, there, Mrs. Cudahy, a lovely morning, is it not?" Bill's hypocritical greetings and *sotto voce* asides were clearly patterned on his mother.

His nasal drawl, on the other hand, was a heritage from his father, who owned an elderly nag named White Swan and made a scanty living hawking fresh vegetables from door to door, which he advertised in a hoarse adenoidal voice. Much against his will, young Bill was forced to accompany his father in the grocery wagon and help peddle the produce. He devoted his efforts to mimicking the elder Dukenfield, chanting in the same singsong whine a list of vegetables which he invented because he liked the names: "Pomegranates, rutabagas, calabashes." When housewives hurried out to purchase these exotics, his father would explain that his son was new to the job, and then clout him on the ear when they were out of sight.

Mr. Dukenfield was a firm believer in strict discipline, and whacked his son regularly whether he deserved it or not. He had lost the little finger of his left hand in the Crimean War — or so Bill claimed — and the absence of this digit made his backhand blow a particularly bruising weapon. Once, at the age of nine, Bill sneaked past the ticket-taker at the local vaudeville house, and spent a fascinated afternoon watching a juggling act. Filled with enthusiasm, he stole some lemons and oranges from his father's cart, and practiced the new art. "By the time I learned to keep two of them in the air at once," he admitted, "I'd ruined several dollars' worth of fruit." His father took stern measures to cure him of this expensive habit, concealing himself in the stable until he caught his son in the act which would one day make him famous, and giving him a parental beating. One afternoon Bill left a small rake in the yard, and when Mr. Dukenfield stepped on it the handle banged his shin. Seeing that Bill was observing him from the doorway with evident amusement, he picked up the rake and bashed it over the boy's head. Bill resolved to square accounts — "I rejected certain measures which might have elicited the attention of the coroner," he said — and settled on the simple solution of hiding on a ledge above the stable door, poising a heavy wooden crate. His father entered, Bill flattened him, and left home at the age of eleven, never to return.

Psychologists have analyzed the humor of W. C. Fields, and concluded that his prejudices and fears were due to a basic hostility toward his father. Mr. Dukenfield was given to singing sentimental ballads around the house, they point out; Bill hated vocal music to his dying day. His cantankerous nature, his never-ending war with producers and directors, indicated a subconscious rebellion against the paternal image. Well, maybe it's all

W. C. Fields as a young man.
(Courtesy of Dave Chasen.)

true, and yet I feel with E. B. White that "Humor can be dissected, as a frog can, but the thing dies in the process and the innards are discouraging to any but the pure scientific mind." Personally I prefer to think of Fields as a comic genius who defies analysis, unequaled among America's funnymen, the one and only.

Gene Buck, who hired Fields for the *Follies,* wrote after his death: "He was amazing and unique, the strangest guy I ever knew in my lifetime. He was all by himself. Nobody could be like him, and a great many tried. He was so damn different, original and talented. He never was a happy guy. He couldn't be, but what color and daring in this game of life! He made up a lot of new rules about everything: conduct, people, morals, entertainment, friendship, gals, pals, fate and happiness, and he had the courage to ignore old rules. . . . He had taken a terrible kicking around in life, and he was tough, bitter, and cynical in an odd humorous way. His gifts and talents as an entertainer were born in him, I think. God made him funny. He knew more about comedy and real humor than any other person. . . . When Bill left the other day, something great in the world died, and something very badly needed."

He had the round ruddy face of a dignified and slightly felonious country squire. Its most prominent feature was the celebrated red-veined nose, which would grow redder like a warning light if he felt he was being victimized. When an insurance company doctor examined him and refused to renew his health policy, he protested to Gene Fowler, "The nefarious quack claimed he found urine in my whisky." His very appearance evoked shouts of laughter from an audience: the manorial air that was so obviously false, the too benign smile, the larcenous eye.

"His whole manner suggested fakery in its most flagrant form," Robert Lewis Taylor wrote in a recent biography. "One of the stills from 'My Little Chickadee' shows him as Cuthbert J. Twillie, a crooked oil man, in a Western poker game with several desperadoes, all eying him appraisingly. Fields himself is rigged out in a cutaway, striped trousers, and a high gray felt hat with a broad black band; he is wearing formal white gloves, which are turned back delicately, and he has a wilted lily in his buttonhole. His hands, graceful and expressive, are carefully shielding his cards from any possible snooping by the man on his left, while his own furtive, suspicious gaze is plainly directed into the hand of the player on his right. His attitude is so frankly dishonest that the other players seem to sense the inevitability of their financial downfall." Their fears were justified in the ensuing scene in which Fields managed to deal himself four aces and win a thousand-dollar pot without having undergone the inconvenience of putting up any money himself.

Fields's distrust of doctors and lawyers was neurotic. "They're all knaves and thieves," he insisted to Gene Fowler once. "I know a thief when I see one. When I was young I was the biggest thief at large. I'd steal golf balls, piggy banks of dear little kiddies, or the nozzle off the hose on the rectory lawn." He termed the members of the medical profession "dastardly fee-splitters. When doctors and undertakers meet, they always wink at each other." Bankers were even worse, he held. In order to outwit their cunning designs, he deposited small sums of money in banks scattered all over the country, even stepping off a transcontinental train to open an account in a small town while the engine was taking on water. Some of these accounts were under his own name, but most of them were credited to Figley J. Whitesides or Dr. Otis Guelpe or Larson E. Whipsnade, names which he had accumulated in the course of his travels. Gene Fowler told me once that Bill had over seven hundred bank accounts or safe-deposit boxes in such far-flung cities as London, Paris, Sydney, Cape Town, and Suva. "I think he lost at least fifty thousand dollars in the Berlin bombing," he speculated. Since Fields never took anyone into his confidence about his financial arrangements, and no bankbooks showed up after his death, it is probable that a sizable fortune is still stashed away in various banks under assumed names. Bill insisted that his unique deposit system not only insured him against conniving bankers, but also made it difficult for income tax agents to collect revenue for the government, which he likewise mistrusted. "Uncle Whiskers will strike down even a child and take away its marbles," he glowered.

Children were another of Fields's pet phobias. "Of course I like little tots," he would protest righteously, "if they're well cooked." When a group of noisy young autograph seekers surrounded him after John Barrymore's funeral, he bellowed, "Get away from me, you diminutive gamins. For two cents — or even one — I'd kick in your teeth. Back to reform school!" His radio feud with Edgar Bergen's wooden dummy, Charlie McCarthy, was genuine, and he would put real feeling into a snarled threat: "I'll slash you into Venetian blinds." Baby LeRoy, with whom he made several films, was his particular aversion. He was convinced that the infant was deliberately plotting to steal scenes from him, and would eye him with dark suspicion, muttering vague threats under his breath. Once he succeeded in spiking Baby LeRoy's orange juice with a surreptitious shot of gin, and sat back amiably while Norman Taurog, the director, tried in vain to rouse the youngster from his pleasant slumbers. "Walk him around, walk him around," Fields advised professionally from a corner. When Baby LeRoy had to be taken home and the shooting postponed till the next day, Fields was jubilant. "That kid's no trouper," he jeered.

One of the most agreeable moments in his film career occurred while shooting *The Old Fashioned Way,* in the course of which Baby LeRoy dropped Fields's watch in the molasses, overturned some soup in his lap, and hit him between the eyes with a spoonful of ice cream. In the following scene, Fields was alone in a room with the obstreperous infant, who was creeping on all four across the carpet. Following the script, his face shining with benevolence, he drew back his foot and lofted his tormentor several feet forward. The cameras recorded some excellent footage, but Fields's conscience evidently troubled him, for the next day he arrived on the set with an armload of toys and gifts for young LeRoy. "One of the gifts was a bowie knife," he chuckled to me malevolently.

Sometimes Bill would lapse into a sentimental mood. "When I was a little tot," he recalled one evening at Chasen's, "I had to earn my way into the circus by lugging water for the elephants. All day long I would trudge back and forth, staggering under the weight of the burdensome receptacles till my arms were numb. Then and there I made a vow that, if I ever succeeded in life, I would donate a sum of money to help some other little tot like myself who had to lug water all day. Waal," and Bill made the gesture of peeling an imaginary glove off his hand and shrugged modestly, "fate proved kind to me, I was blest with more than my share of life's riches, and one day I thought of the money I'd vowed to give that poor little tot lugging water." His eyes narrowed. "And then I had a second thought: f—— him."

Strangely his language, though generously larded with obscenities, never seemed off-color or offensive. Today's degenerate jokes and sick humor are, to me, infinitely more filthy than Bill's earthy Anglo-Saxon speech. His drawling voice and squirelike dignity robbed a four-letter word of any suggestion of smut. On stage, of course, he resorted to euphemisms like "Drat!" or "Godfrey Daniel!" to elude the censor; but the truth is that Fields was genuinely embarrassed by dirty stories, particularly when told in the presence of women. If someone started a bawdy anecdote in mixed company, he would make some excuse to leave the room, or wander around uneasily in a pretended search for a match.

Fields's attitude toward women was courtly, even a trifle old-fashioned, and he would remove his hat punctiliously in an elevator or rise promptly to his feet if a lady entered the room. One hot afternoon Bill was sitting stark naked behind his desk when Billy Grady and a female companion burst through the door without warning. Ever the gentleman, Bill stood up politely and extended his hand, and then blinked in surprise as the lady gasped and departed in haste. He greeted members of the fair sex with such cavalier terms of endearment as "My little chickadee" or "My glow-worm" or, in a romantic scene with Mae West, "My little brood mare." At the time his residence on Toluca Lake was up for sale, Fields volunteered to show a timid pair of prospective purchasers around the house. "This is the dining room," he explained as they started their tour, "and this is the library, and this is the mah-ster bedroom." He led them across his room, past the rumpled bed where a blonde was lying asleep on her stomach. "How are you, my little turtle-dove?" he inquired, patting her fanny solicitously. "And this," he continued with perfect poise to the speechless couple, "is the sun-porch. . . ."

It was his dislike of birds — still another of Bill's innumerable prejudices — which led him to sell his Toluca Lake home, an imposing mansion with broad green lawns sloping down to an artificial lake, the featured attraction of the real estate development. The shallow lake was populated by numerous ducks and swans, which used to roam over Bill's property and hiss at him, an unforgivable affront to an actor. Whenever Bill spotted one of his web-footed adversaries cropping his grass, he would place a golf ball in position and drive it accurately at the intruder with a number-four iron, whereupon the outraged bird

would flap its wings and chase Bill up the lawn and into the
house. The battle grew more and more ruthless. Once Bill
borrowed a canoe and pursued a large swan all over the lake,
until he dozed off after his strenuous efforts, and the swan crept
up behind the canoe and nipped him from the rear. "The
miscreant fowl broke all the rules of civilized warfare," he
complained later.

Norm McLeod, who lived two doors away, was directing him
in a picture for Paramount, and was well aware of Bill's
reputation for being taken drunk in the middle of the shooting.
To make sure that nothing happened, McLeod moved from his
own home and spent each watchful night on a cot in Bill's
bedroom. One Sunday morning Norm slept late, and awoke
with a start to find his roommate missing. As he leaped off the
cot, his bare foot collided with an empty Bourbon bottle, and he
suspected the worst. Somewhere in the distance he could hear
Bill's voice, but he had a little trouble locating it. At last he
stepped out onto the sun-porch, which commanded a sweeping
view of Toluca Lake and the surrounding estates, their bedroom
windows wide open in the early Sabbath stillness. Fields, clad in
pajamas and carpet slippers, was wandering around the grass,
liberally dotted with unsightly white droppings deposited by the
ducks and swans. Grasping a heavy cane by the stick end, he was
swinging it right and left at the feathered trespassers, bellowing
in a voice which must have penetrated every neighboring
boudoir, "If you can't shit green, get off my lawn."

Bill's capacity for alcohol was enormous — his household
staff estimated that he consumed two quarts of Martinis a
day — but I never saw him show the slightest effect. "I have a
system," he confided to me once. "I know I've had enough
when my knees bend backward." Although pictured by the
public as a lush who indulged in wild drinking sprees, Fields
had nothing but contempt for the thick-tongued staggering

drunk, and would order a friend from his house if he became tipsy. "Gives drinking a bad name," he growled. His own day started with a modest breakfast of two Martinis (if ravenous, he would take a third), and lunch consisted of another couple of Martinis which he washed down with some heavily re-inforced imported beer. He brought a giant foam-rubber ice bucket of Martinis each day to the studio, the rear of his car was converted into an efficient bar, and he would secrete a dozen miniatures in the pockets of his golf bag before setting out for an afternoon on the links. "I always keep a supply of stimulant handy in case I see a snake," he liked to explain, "which I also keep handy." Generally this would tide him over until the cocktail hour before dinner. "Don't believe in eating on an empty stomach," he maintained.

Alcohol seemed to serve as a sedative for his jangled nerves, and put him in a relaxed mood for a performance. "His timing was better when he was drinking," Mack Sennett claimed. "He was sharp, sure, positive." Every so often, after a hospital siege, he would determine to give up drinking entirely. During one of these periods, we met at Chasen's before going to the opening of the *Ice Follies,* and Bill announced that he was on the wagon. On the wagon, I discovered, meant that he had given up Martinis, and drank only Bourbon and Scotch and beer and brandy. As a result of his abstinence, we did not finish dinner until ten-thirty, and the *Ice Follies* were almost over when we arrived. Even the usual crowd of autograph hunters outside the theater had dispersed, save for one pimply youngster who spotted Fields as he descended from his limousine and ran across the sidewalk, holding out a notebook and pleading, "C'n I have your autograph, Mr. Fields?" "Why, of course, of course, yaas, to be sure," Bill said pleasantly, and inscribed his name with a flourish. The boy stammered his thanks, and Bill patted him fondly on the head. "Quite all right, my nose-picking little bastard," he pronounced in benediction, and entered the theater.

Billy Grady, who had managed Fields's business affairs during his early career, assured me one night at dinner that Bill always traveled with two wardrobe trunks, one for clothes and one for gin. "That's a lie," Fields thundered, "I had gin in both trunks." Fields and Grady loved to tell stories of their road trips together, interrupting each other repeatedly with blistering insults. "One night in Homosassa, Florida," Bill began. "It was Ocala, Florida, you feeble-minded moron," Grady broke in. "You call everything Homosassa because you like the name." "Keep your Irish-Catholic mouth shut," Bill roared back, and turned to me. "One night in Homosassa, Florida, we were driving in the rain when I spotted a man with a satchel standing under a street light, signaling for a lift. I requested Grady to halt our vehicle and let the stranger climb aboard —"

"I'm the one who wanted to stop for him, you kindergarten dropout," Grady interrupted. "You were afraid he'd drink some of your gin."

Fields gave him a withering glance. "Out of the goodness of my heart, I proffered the fellow a touch of stimulant to ward off a chill, and he gave me a look of righteous indignation. 'Look not upon the wine when it is red,' he said, 'It stingeth like the adder, and biteth like the serpent. Eschew the curse of the demon rum.'

"I motioned Grady to pull up at the side of the road. 'Who are you, my good man?' I inquired.

" 'I am a minister of the gospel,' he said, opening his satchel and taking out some religious tracts, 'and it is my duty to convert you from the evils of drink.'

" 'Out, you pious son-of-a-bitch, out!' I said, and placing my foot against his chest I propelled him backward into a drainage ditch, pausing only to toss an empty gin bottle into the ditch

beside him before we drove on." Bill shuddered at the recollection. "A most unnerving experience," he sighed, and signaled
the waiter to replenish his glass.

Bill had first won fame as "The Tramp Juggler," developing
the skill he had acquired with his father's oranges and lemons
into a spectacular vaudeville act which he climaxed by juggling
twenty-five cigar boxes balanced end on end with a rubber ball
on top. He employed no patter, causing *Variety* to observe:
"Why Mr. Fields does not speak is quite simple. His comedy
speaks for him." As his reputation grew, Gene Buck signed him
for the *Ziegfeld Follies of 1915,* part of a glittering cast which
included Ann Pennington and George White, Bert Williams,
Ina Claire, and Ed Wynn as "Himself." It was in the *Follies*
that Fields introduced Broadway to his immortal pool-table act,
using an ancient billiard cue warped and twisted into a spiral.
He would sight dubiously along the cue, halt his game to shift
the chalk a few critical inches right or left because it offended
his expert eye, and give the racked balls a single whack. An
ingenious system of concealed strings would yank the balls into
the pockets like a colony of gophers taking cover. After a heated
session, in which he ripped the felt cloth into shreds, he would
rear on tiptoes for a final killing shot and drive the cue
downward through the splintered table, plunging his arm into
the hole up to the shoulder.

Ed Wynn and Fields, as rival comedians, were constantly
vying for laughs. During one performance, Wynn concealed
himself beneath the pool table and tried to steal the scene by
smirking and winking at the audience. Fields became uneasily
aware that his laughs were coming at the wrong places, and his
eye caught a suspicious movement under the table. He waited
patiently until Wynn, on all fours, carelessly stuck his head out
too far. With a juggler's perfect timing, Fields swung the butt
end of his cue in a half-circle and lowered it onto his rival's

skull. Wynn sagged to the floor while Fields continued his game serenely amid boisterous applause. Every time that Wynn struggled back to consciousness and emitted a low moan, the audience laughed louder at what they thought was his clever impersonation. Later Fields suggested that Wynn's bit might be incorporated into the act each night for the duration of the run, but Wynn declined to take advantage of his offer.

During his successive years in the *Follies* — Fields appeared in every edition from 1915 through 1921 — he created other comic routines which have become famous: the golf act, in which a stray piece of paper blew across the course and wrapped itself inextricably around his club, defying all his efforts to shake it off; the rear of a three-story tenement, with Fields trying in vain to take a nap in a porch hammock amid the bedlam of neighborhood noises; the subway scene in the 1921 *Follies,* in which he was supported by Fannie Brice, Raymond Hitchcock, and Ray Dooley as a howling infant. Gradually Fields was building the familiar character of a frustrated man, harassed by inanimate objects over which he had no control — much the same beleaguered citizen portrayed, in a different technique, by Robert Benchley. His characterization reached perfection in 1923 with the musical comedy *Poppy,* in which the former Tramp Juggler graduated once and for all into an authentic and expert comedian. Fields played the role of Eustace McGargle, a magnificent fraud who gained his livelihood by fleecing the local yokels at a country fair. The grandiose eloquence and unctuous smile of the unscrupulous mountebank, urging the innocent farmers to participate with him in the shell-game and then commenting in an aside, "Never give a sucker an even break," established the pattern which Fields followed the rest of his life.

*Poppy* was an enormous success, and Bill, in a tender moment, brought his mother from Philadelphia to New York to watch his performance. "Why, Claude, I didn't know you had such a good memory," was Mrs. Dukenfield's cryptic comment. At a midnight supper after the show, Bill regaled her with hair-raising tales of his travels among savage tribes in the South Pacific. "One night some aborigines invited me to dinner," he began, "a tasty repast, starting off with whale —"

"Gracious," Mrs. Dukenfield interrupted, "I should think that would have been a meal in itself."

Fields's film debut occurred in 1925 at the Paramount Studios on Long Island. Paramount had decided to make a silent motion picture of *Poppy* — which was retitled, for obscure reasons, *Sally of the Sawdust* — and, after trying vainly to engage Fatty Arbuckle for the part of Eustace McGargle, reluctantly hired Fields to play his original stage role. Fields, giving the industry a foretaste of what it might expect in future years, usurped the star's dressing room, bullied D. W. Griffith, the director, and generally ran things with a high hand. Since Fields had created the McGargle character and could play it in his sleep, the picture was hailed as a comic masterpiece, and he followed it in 1926 with *So's Your Old Man,* and a year later with *Running Wild,* both directed by Gregory La Cava.

Although they struck sparks from the start — Fields always referred to him as "that dago bastard" — La Cava became a lifelong friend. Out of their intimate association, La Cava formed the theory that Fields's whole life was dedicated to repaying society for his cruel childhood. Robert Lewis Taylor quotes La Cava: "Nearly everything Bill tried to get into his movies was something that lashed out at the world. The peculiar thing is that although he thought he was being pretty mean there wasn't any real sting to it. It was only funny. Bill never really wanted to hurt anybody. He just felt an obligation."

Fields had the divine ability to turn his prejudices to comic advantage. Since acquiring a car, he had developed a persecution complex about road hogs, who he was convinced were out to get him, and would drive with one wary eye on the oncoming lane of traffic, ready for any hostile vehicle to attack him. His sequence in *If I Had a Million* gratified a lifelong thirst for vengeance. With the million dollars which he inherited, he purchased a number of secondhand cars and hired a flock of intrepid drivers, and he and Alison Skipworth set forth at the head of the column, his eye peeled for the first offender to cut across the center line. When he spotted a culprit, he would hold up a hand and signal one of his commandos to wheel out and ram it. Sometimes he and Miss Skipworth would take part in the fray, and Fields would give a bloodcurdling yell of exultation as headlights shattered and wheels came off and fenders crumpled.

His enmity toward children, dating from his own persecuted boyhood, found expression in *Never Give a Sucker an Even Break*, written by Fields himself under the unlikely nom de plume of Otis Criblecoblis. In one gratifying bit with Gloria Jean, as his little niece, Bill lured the child into a saloon and plied her with an opaque fluid which he assured her was goat's milk. "What kind of goat's milk, Uncle Bill?" Gloria asked after a delectable sip.

"Nanny goat's milk, my dear," the doting uncle replied, absently flicking a cigarette lighter as he expelled his breath and sending a long sheet of flame across the bar.

Bill's pictures violated every known moral code, and endorsed such dubious enterprises as swindling, theft, and other degrading aspects of human nature. In *The Bank Dick,* which he wrote under his alternate pen name of Mahatma Kane Jeeves, he not only defied conventions, but reaped all the rewards of dishonesty. The plot, if it could be called that, concerned one Egbert Sousé (Fields insisted on the accent over the *e*) who was trying to acquire five hundred dollars to invest in a beefsteak mine. A couple of robbers, Filthy McNasty and Repulsive Rogan, held up the local bank; but as they fled with the loot McNasty stumbled over a park bench where Sousé was seated and knocked himself out. Sousé modestly explained to the bank president that he had subdued the miscreant at a great personal risk — "He pulled an assagai on me," he claimed — and was rewarded with the job of bank dick. His first official act was to capture a small boy carrying a water pistol.

The plot rambled on with dreamlike nonsequitur through a series of unrelated episodes, including one wildly extraneous sequence in which Fields discovered a movie company on location, and took over the sedan of the director, labeled A. Pismo Clam, to shoot a football sequence. In another episode, he escorted the bank examiner, J. Pinkerton Snoopington (beautifully played by Franklin Pangborn), into the Black Pussy Cat Café and Snack Bar, his favorite saloon, and asked the bartender pointedly, "Have you seen Michael Finn lately?" While the unsuspecting Snoopington was swallowing his Mickey, Fields ordered himself a Scotch with water on the side, downed it, washed his fingers delicately in the water glass, and asked for another Scotch with a fresh chaser. "Never like to bathe in the same water twice," he remarked. Eventually Fields struck a bonanza in the beefsteak mine; and the final scene showed Mr. Sousé, having triumphed over virtue, placing his hat absentmindedly on his upended cane and setting off in the direction of the saloon, unregenerate to the end.

Bill was fascinated by unusual names, adding new ones to his collection as he came across them. "Every name I use is an actual one I've seen somewhere," he told Norman Taurog. "Posthewhistle & Smunn, Attorneys" was borrowed from a Philadelphia law firm; "Claude Nesselrode" was a local pugilist who took frequent dives at Jeffries' Barn; "Chester Snavely" was an undertaker he had known as a boy in Germantown;

W. C. Fields as a pugilist.
(Courtesy of Dave Chasen.)

"Chester Bogle," the pseudonym he used when writing *You Can't Cheat an Honest Man,* was a bootlegger of his acquaintance. He insisted on authoring his own screen plays, which he would dash off on the back of an old grocery bill and then sell to the studio for twenty-five thousand dollars. Since his contract specified that he had story approval, he would notify the studio that he had rejected the script, and compose a second one for another twenty-five thousand dollars. (Norman McLeod told me that Fields once built up his total take on a single story to eighty-five thousand dollars.) After the script was finally approved and paid for, he would toss it aside and ad-lib on the set as he went along.

His cantankerous attitude toward producers and directors worsened as he became a leading Hollywood star. He refused to sign a lucrative contract with Paramount until he was given complete autonomy in the preparation, direction, and production of his films. When he moved to M-G-M, he was barely prevented from taking over the studio. Directors raved and ranted at his proclivity for altering scenes or inserting new comic routines — when he played the role of Mr. Micawber in *David Copperfield,* he wanted to work in a juggling act, and it took all the studio's efforts to dissuade him — but it must be said that Fields, a consummate craftsman and master of clownery, knew more about his own capabilities than any director. He was equally rebellious during his radio appearances on the "Lucky Strike" program, and kept referring to his son "Chester" for several weeks, until his sponsors belatedly realized that "Chester Fields" might indicate a rival product.

If he failed to have his say, he would stage a one-man strike and sulk until the studio came around to his way of thinking. During the shooting of a picture at M-G-M, he was rebuffed on some minor change (he wanted his name to have top billing above that of the studio) and retired to his residence, leaving orders with his butler to tell any and all callers that he was not at home. As the set lay idle day after day and production costs mounted, a series of executives drove out to see him, but were turned away from his door. At last L. B. Mayer, the head of the studio, decided to make a personal visit. The butler opened the door and recognized the distinguished caller, and left him standing in the hallway while he hurried back to Fields's bedroom for instructions. "It's L.B. himself," he whispered nervously to the master. "What shall I say to him?"

"Give him an eva-a-asive answer," Fields drawled. "Tell him to go f—— himself."

Of all the houses that Fields occupied while in Hollywood, his favorite was a run-down Spanish mansion on De Mille Drive, north of Hollywood. He had leased it during the depression for the bargain price of $250 a month, including the services of a Japanese gardener. When conditions improved, the landlord tried in vain to persuade his tenant to change the long-term lease, but Fields gloated over his advantage and refused to yield. The unhappy landlord suggested a compromise, and offered to renovate the old house if his tenant would agree to a financial readjustment. "Not one cent for tribute," Fields bellowed. "Let the joint fall apart."

The situation was a stalemate, and since neither tenant nor owner would invest in repairs, the mansion became more and more down-at-heel in appearance. The wallpaper hung in tatters, the warp of the carpet showed plainly before the three bars which Fields had installed, and chunks of plaster occasionally fell from the sagging ceiling onto the pool table he had set up in the drawing room. The living room was given over to a Ping-Pong table, and high pool-room chairs were arranged along the walls. The dining room featured a barber's chair, complete with towels and aprons, in which Bill used to doze when troubled by insomnia. (In his early days, he had found

that getting a haircut in a warm padded barber's chair was one
of life's greatest pleasures.) With his native distrust of servants,
he had fitted every closet and storeroom door with a special lock
to guard his liquor supply, and kept some thirty keys on a chain
in his bathrobe pocket. His upstairs bedroom, which he called
his "office," contained a combination bar and writing desk and
bed, with slats like a crib to keep him from falling out. When
his steps grew feeble, he would feel his way from his bed along
the desk to the bar, and reinforce his strength with a handy
nightcap.

He had an abiding fear of burglars, and his solution, of
which he was inordinately proud, was the installation of an
intercom system throughout the house, with the master microphone on the desk in his office. Loudspeakers were concealed
everywhere, in the pantry, down in the cellar, inside chandeliers,
under washbasins, behind pictures, and back of the knocker on
the front door, a carved woodpecker which the guest activated
by yanking a string. If he heard a suspicious noise during the
night, he would grope to the desk and pick up the microphone
and bellow into it, "Stand back, I've got you covered!" and then
go back to bed, confident that the intruder would remain with
arms raised until morning.

During the war, on my way out to the Pacific on Air Force
duty, I stopped off in Los Angeles and took a cab out to De
Mille Drive. The approach to Bill's house was a red-tiled lane,
overhung with flowered trellises, and the velvet lawns, well
tended by the Japanese gardener, rolled gently down the con-
tour of the hill to form a bowl with a lily pond in the center.
On it was floating a toy sailboat, a gift from one of Fields's
friends. I stepped up to the door and reached for the string of
the knocker, and the woodpecker yelled, *"Let* go of me, Ford!"
in Bill's snarling voice. (He had a telescope in his office, I
learned later, with which he could spot any approaching visi-

tor.) He came downstairs, clad in his disreputable white bathrobe and holding a tall glass filled with a yellowish liquid. I
had heard that Bill's health was failing, and I assumed that his
drinking had been restricted to wine. We adjourned to the
outdoor patio, one of Bill's preferred spots, and he bellowed to
the butler, "Bring my guest a Scotch highball — and I'll have
another Martini." He drank four shakerfuls of Martinis during
my visit, and his good humor expanded. I had never seen him in
a happier mood. Once the landlord stopped by, to inquire about
the month's rent which was overdue, and Bill assured him
loftily, "Have no qualms, my good man, your pound of flesh
will be forthcoming shortly. *Good* day," and then, in a croaked
aside like a honk of a raven, "All landlords should be grilled *en
brochette.*" At last it came time to leave, and Bill presented me
with an affectionately inscribed photograph of himself, not in
clown costume but in street attire with his face turned toward
the camera so that his oversized nose did not show. I've never
known what impulse prompted him to give me his picture. I
made my way carefully up the uneven tile walk, for my knees
were beginning to bend backward, and he waved his glass to me
gaily as I reached the gate. It was the last time I ever saw him.

I returned to Hollywood shortly before Christmas of 1946,
and Dave Chasen told me that Bill had lost the De Mille Drive
house, when his lease expired, and had moved to a sanitarium in
Los Encinas to sit in a rocking chair and await the Man in the
Bright Nightgown. Dave and Billy Grady planned to drive out
to see him on Christmas Day, a holiday which Fields always
loathed. "I believed in Christmas until I was eight years old,"
he told Gene Fowler. "I had saved up some money carrying ice
in Philadelphia, and I was going to buy my mother a copper-
bottom clothes boiler for Christmas. I kept the money hidden in
a brown crock in the coalbin. My father found the crock. He did
exactly what I would have done in his place. He stole the money.

And ever since then I've remembered nobody on Christmas, and I want nobody to remember me either."

Dave promised to take me along to Los Encinas on his next visit. "Bill isn't allowed any callers," he said, "but we'll manage to get in somehow." That was when I realized how seriously ill he was. On Christmas there was a tropical deluge, which flooded the streets with such a boiling torrent that a man stepped out of his car and was swept into a sewer and drowned. ("Rain dampens sidewalks in Los Angeles area," the Los Angeles *Times* admitted grudgingly the next day.) Somehow I kept thinking of Bill all day. It was just the kind of Christmas he would have chosen.

Dave phoned me late that afternoon. He and Billy Grady had arrived at the sanitarium about noon, he said, with a hamper of delicacies from the restaurant and several bottles of whiskey. They made their way through the downpour to Bill's bungalow, and Dave rang the bell and then knelt down, a simple gag designed to startle the party opening the door. A nurse answered the bell, weeping. "Mr. Fields died this morning," she said. Dave climbed to his feet in silence, and they drove back to Hollywood in the gray rain. That night some of Bill's intimates gathered at Chasen's, and phoned a full-page ad to the *Hollywood Reporter:*

The most prejudiced and honest and beloved figure of our so-called "colony" went away on a day that he pretended to abhor — "Christmas." We loved him, and — peculiarly enough — he loved us. To the most authentic humorist since Mark Twain, to the greatest heart that has beaten since the Middle Ages — W. C. Fields, our friend.

Several weeks after his death, a group of his closest friends met at Chasen's for a wake: Billy Grady, Eddie Sutherland, Ben Hecht, Grantland Rice, Greg La Cava, Gene Fowler, Jack

Dempsey, Roland Young, Leo McCarey, Norm McLeod. Dave served us Bill's favorite dinner, accompanied by Bill's usual quota of drinks. None of us could keep up with it, and my recollection of the evening is still hazy. I remember that, by some unexpressed agreement, no one at the table mentioned Bill's name; that wasn't necessary. The only reference to him was when Dave read aloud a telegram he had just received from Frank Sullivan in New York.

I HOPE HE GIVES ST. PETER AN EVASIVE ANSWER, the wire said.

# 11

## *Salt Water Taffy*

M Y John Riddell parodies were brought out in book form
by Charles Scribner's Sons, whose editorial chief, Max-
well Perkins, was another of the six great editors I've known
in my life. (Since I've mentioned this mythical list several
times, I may as well name them now and have done with all
the suspense. They are: Harold Ross of *The New Yorker,*
Frank Crowninshield of *Vanity Fair,* Charles Colebaugh of
*Collier's,* Ben Hibbs of the *Saturday Evening Post,* DeWitt
Wallace of the *Reader's Digest,* and Max Perkins. And a
seventh would be Harold Ober, my literary agent for many
years, whose infallible judgment and taste and rigid integrity
made him the greatest editor of them all.)

Max Perkins was slight and hollow-chested, with a pinched
face and tight Calvin Coolidge lips which made him seem older
than his years, and a voice like scuffed autumn leaves. One of
his eccentricities was to stand all day at an upright school-
master's desk in his office, correcting manuscripts and signing
letters with, I always suspected, a goose quill pen. He preferred
to work with his hat on, chain-smoked cigarettes, and looked on
the telephone as an anachronistic intrusion in the world of

letters. At the end of each afternoon, he would adjourn business to the Men's Bar at the old Ritz, settle himself in his special red-leather chair by the window, and sip Martinis with the devotion of W. C. Fields himself while he discussed ideas with one or another of his authors. His serene humor, sardonic and bone-dry, enabled him to cope with the erratic geniuses in his stable.

Scribner's published many of the leading writers of the Twenties, and Max handled them all with tact and understanding. Even the morose Ring Lardner brightened under the spell of his warm enthusiasm. He edited the vast slovenly manu-scripts of Thomas Wolfe, and revised them with infinite pa-tience into some semblance of form. Scott Fitzgerald was his special concern, and if necessary he would chaperone Scott during a bibulous night on the town, sitting in a nightclub like a prim duenna until his temperamental charge was ready to be led home. It was in Max's office that the exhibitionistic Ernest Hemingway staged his notorious fistfight with Max Eastman. (Eastman had intimated in a review that Hemingway had no hair on his chest, and Hemingway, peeling off his shirt to display his hirsute adornment, engaged his critic in battle until Max Perkins broke it up.) Hemingway's insistence on using obscenities in his books was a constant source of concern to his conservative publishers. Max confided to me once that elderly Charles Scribner, perusing the manuscript of *Death in the Afternoon,* decided that one recurrent four-letter word would have to be deleted, and jotted it down on a memo pad and stuck it on the spike as he went out to lunch, intending to discuss it with Max later. His secretary, straightening his desk in his absence, read the memo and sighed, "My God, do I have to remind the old man about that, too?"

Even as dignified a house as Scribner's yielded now and then to the prevalent craze for literary teas and autograph parties and other promotional whoopdedoo. One of my collections, called

*The John Riddell Murder Case,* was shaped as an overall parody
of the popular series of "Murder Cases" by S. S. Van Dine, the
pseudonym of Willard Huntington Wright, who was also
published by Scribner's. Van Dine (as Wright perferred to be
called) and I were requested by the publicity department to
make a number of joint public appearances, which proved to be
somewhat spotty due to Van Dine's addiction to Napoleon
brandy. Once at the National Arts Club he passed out cold on
the platform during the introductions, and I was left to debate
with myself. On another occasion we were guests at the annual
banquet of the Princeton *Tiger,* and again he missed the dinner
entirely. The evening was not altogether wasted, however, for I
met the *Tiger*'s young art editor, son of Scribner's business
manager Whitney Darrow, who was later to become a leading
*New Yorker* cartoonist and illustrator of one of my books.

Those latter Twenties — the Ballyhoo Years, Frederick
Lewis Allen called them in *Only Yesterday* — saw the emer-
gence of the promoter in all his glory. The up-and-coming new
phenomenon called radio had linked the country together, so
that a skillful publicity agent could build a minor event into a
coast-to-coast sensation. "One of the striking characteristics of
the era of Coolidge Prosperity," Allen wrote, "was the un-
paralleled rapidity and unanimity with which millions of men
and women turned their attention, their talk, and their emotional interest upon a series of tremendous trifles." People
ignored the important issues of the day in favor of the lurid
scandal, the bizarre disaster, the get-rich-quick scheme. The
medicine men of advertising whipped the nation into a froth
over the real estate boom in Florida, and even former Secretary
of State William Jennings Bryan hired out as a barker for Coral
Gables, extolling the local climate in mellifluous tones while
Gilda Gray did the shimmy on the same platform. The services
for Rudolph Valentino were exploited by the press agent for

column was started. Who knows how many more copies before it
~er? Millions, anyway. Max, telephone for you.

nd the Inner Shrine wants to state that this autobiography by
~per Joan (471,002 just now, Dick, or I'm lying to you. Bren-
's.) is an absolutely true and authentic account of her life at sea,
~ the exception maybe of one or two minor discrepancies, such as
~use of the word "sea" instead of "land." Just hold the wire,
~se, Mr. Colcord.

~ven though Joan Riddell has altered a few insignificant facts,
~ as the fact that she wrote it — how can I give this out to the
~rs when my poor head is buzzing with figures, 769,029 before
~ could say Trader Horn — the essential integrity cannot be
~ally impaired — 989,996 copies, yi, yi, one million and we raise
~rice. Lincoln, the Book-of-the-Month Club wants to know if we
~nother good book for them next month.

~nyway, what does the public want for $2.75 — the truth?

~e parody began, in Miss Lowell's style, with a bit of verse:

Rockabye, Joan, publicity's swell.
 While the wind blows, the "Cradle" will sell.
 When the news breaks, the "Cradle" will fall,
  And down will come Simon, Schuster and all . . ."
                    — *Old South Sea Chantey*

~ou see this here fish, Joan? This here fish is called a sucker. It's
~ a sucker because it will swallow anything. There are hundreds
~ousands of these suckers, Joan, most of them belonging to the
~of-the-Month Club. It's just one more of the mysteries of the

~as old Britches talking, and he was explaining to me some of
~ysteries of the sea while I lay curled upstairs in the mizzen
~ of my father's schooner, trying to reef a gaff tops'l. Old
~es was also responsible for teaching me many other mysteries of
~, such as how I could attend high school in California while I
~ the South Seas, and how my father's ship could burn three

Frank Campbell's Funeral Parlor with such rabble-rousing
effect that Broadway was jammed for eleven blocks and scores
of weeping females were injured in the mob riot. So effective
was the tub-thumping over the second Dempsey-Tunney heavyweight bout that the staid New York *Times* announced the
result in three-bank headlines across its front page, and five
radio listeners dropped dead at their sets during the thirteen-
second-long count.

Sensationalism sold newspapers, the editors found, and vast
acres of space were devoted to the Leopold-Loeb trial in
Chicago, the Prince of Wales's visit to Long Island, or Balto the
sled dog's heroic dash to bring the serum to Nome. An estimated five million words were dispatched from Somerville,
New Jersey, during the Hall-Mills trial, and the galaxy of
special reporters for this Roman holiday included Mary Roberts
Rinehart, Billy Sunday, and the Reverend John Roach Straton.
The sordid Snyder-Gray murder, a few months later, received
more attention than the sinking of the *Titanic,* and was covered
by such unlikely writers as Peggy Hopkins Joyce and David
Wark Griffith. John Scopes, Floyd Collins, "Red" Grange, and
"Daddy" and "Peaches" Browning became celebrities overnight, and were as quickly forgotten. And on May 20, 1927,
when a stunt pilot flew solo across the Atlantic to win a twenty-
five-thousand-dollar prize, every record for hullabaloo was
shattered and every hyperbole exhausted. The entire population
was united in a wave of mass excitement like a revival meeting,
forty thousand boxing fans stood with bared heads in Yankee
Stadium to pray for Lindbergh, George M. Cohan wrote a song
about "Lucky Lindy," and the New York *Evening World* stated
editorially that the modest young flier had performed "the
greatest feat of a solitary man in the records of the human
race." After almost two weeks of incessant headlines, Benchley
sent a cable to his friend Charles Brackett in Paris: HAVE YOU

HEARD ANY NEWS OF LINDBERGH? LEFT HERE TEN DAYS AGO. AM WORRIED. Brackett wired back: DO YOU MEAN GEORGE LINDBERGH?

Inevitably the promotion racket spread to the publishing business. In my book-review column in *Vanity Fair,* early in 1929, I complained sourly that "once upon a time publishers wore white goatees, spoke English, and took some slight pride in what appeared under the imprint of their houses. All that has been swept aside. Today book production in America is a mad scramble for bigger and better best sellers; a merry-go-round of publicity stunts, propaganda gags, pep lunches for the critics, paid testimonials, blindfold tests of Borzoi books by George Gershwin and the Princess Mayovskaya, blindfold endorsements of Simon and Schuster books by William McFee and Heywood Broun, jacket blurbs by the Professional Hailers' Association; a general acceleration of hokum and bunkum and balderdash, culminating in the recent front-page exposure of the Joan Lowell hoax, an affair which will linger long on the palate as the worst taste of the 1928–1929 publishing season."

A California girl named Joan Lowell had written (conceivably with ghostly assistance) an autobiography called *The Cradle of the Deep,* which told of her seventeen years at sea on her father's ship, the *Minnie A. Caine,* a four-masted windjammer "engaged in the copra and candlewood trade between the islands of the South Seas and Australia." Joan described herself as the only "woman-thing" among a crew of hard-boiled but chivalrous sailors, and told in anatomical detail how she had learned about sex by dissecting a female shark; and Simon and Schuster were quick to see the promotional possibilities. Back in 1924 Dick Simon and Max Schuster had reaped a handsome profit by bringing out the first Cross-Word Puzzle book; later they had successfully parlayed the adventures of an obscure African peddler named Trader Horn into a national best seller;

now they set the drums beating and trum Lowell's salty opus. William McFee and burg, old shellbacks and experts in mar duced to make statements in which they sional reputations that every word of *Th* was true. It was chosen as the March sel the Month Club by its trusting editorial McFee, Dorothy Canfield, Henry Seide Morley, and Heywood Broun, who a accuracy than he realized, that he had be away." Sales in the first month were *Cradle of the Deep* skyrocketed to the top and all was well until a diligent critic r did some digging in educational and discovered that Miss Lowell had been a Junior High School in Berkeley, Califor supposed to be in the South Seas, tha master of the *Minnie A. Caine* for only the ship she described as burning to the tied to a West Coast dock in perfect cond

The controversy was still raging whe in *Vanity Fair* called "Rockabye, Joan," a lampoon of the chatty newspaper Schuster ran under the title "From the I

From the Inner Shri
BUYER and BOOST
*Gold Bricks our Spe*

Such excitement today — 106,337 co Shrine can hardly contain itself — 201,0 Dick, get quick on the wire — in offeri ROCKABYE, JOAN, the new Best Seller b has already sold how many? — 331,056

miles out and still be found tied to a dock ten years later. I was only two or three weeks old, however, and I could hardly have been concerned with these mysteries at my age. After all, they were my publishers' worry and not mine. I was perfectly content just to lie about my father's boat — a habit which has persisted in later life.

I cannot remember when I was not on a ship. (Not here, anyway.) My father was master of the *Minnie A. Caine* for fifteen months, and during this time I managed to spend seventeen years aboard her, from 1909 to 1917. My father taught me all the mathematics I ever knew.

When the *Carrie L. Maine* steamed out of San Francisco harbor, I headed her north across the Pacific toward Australia. (Australia is due north of San Francisco, right next to Spain.) At that time we were engaged in the copra trade among the islands of the South Seas. This was a rather dangerous trade, and indeed my earliest childhood memories are of listening to the vicious copras in the hold, hissing and darting their forked fangs. In exchange for these copras, we used to bring back oakum, which we shipped to America to be used in the manufacture of travel books and sea-stories.

Although I was less than a year old, my father insisted on dressing me in a sou'wester hat and slicker — "just in case some photographers should come aboard," as he used to say — and I did my tricks at the wheel like the rest of the crew. (One of my favorite tricks was to detach the wheel and roll it over the side.) Despite the fact that the sailors of the *Mabel I. Cohen* were always ready to play Post-Office or other kissing games with me, I missed the companionship of children my own age; and to amuse myself I used to invent imaginary trips back home, during which I would pretend that I lived in Berkeley for a number of years and attended the Garfield Junior High School. So real were these visits, in fact, that a number of schoolmates still remember me as a member of the Class of 1918. It is just one more of the mysteries of the sea. . . .

My parody had barely appeared when George Palmer Putnam, head of G. P. Putnam's Sons, phoned to ask if I would

*The Time of Laughter*

expand it into a book. He had already arranged for my release from Scribner's, he said to my surprise. (Later I learned not to be surprised at anything.) Could I deliver completed copy in ten days? That's fine, then. Click.

I suppose the best description of George Palmer Putnam is to say that he was the diametric opposite of Max Perkins. He was tall and wiry and dynamic, with a dark shaven jaw, close-cropped black hair prematurely flecked with gray, an engaging laugh (he was fond of outrageous puns), and a disconcerting habit of accenting his speech now and then with a hollow *clunk!* like a stone dropped down a well, that came from somewhere deep in his nasal passages. His friendly manner was offset by the hard calculating glance behind his steel spectacles. A phrase that John McNulty once used in a story kept recurring to me: "His eye was as cold as an undertaker's night bell."

George Putnam — he was usually called "GP," which was sometimes shortened to "Gyp" — was the past master of literary legerdemain, a skilled conjurer who could palm an author, pull a best seller out of his hat, flourish his wand and transform a channel swimmer or explorer or aviator into a national sensation. With his knack for showmanship, he published the memoirs of page one celebrities who sparkled briefly and then, as they began to fizzle, were discarded for the next headline hero. His staff ghost-writer, Fitzhugh Green, hammered out Lindbergh's autobiography, *We,* so rapidly that copies were ready for distribution before the public welcome had died down. The Martin Johnsons, Captain Bob Bartlett, Admiral Richard Byrd, pilots Clarence Chamberlain and Amelia Earhart were all products of the same razzle-dazzle promotion, captive lions in the Putnam zoo.

His instinct for the spectacular was almost occult. He could sense a news story before it occurred. When another front-page notable popped up, his eyes fairly snapped with electricity, his fingers coiled and writhed like live wires, his voice had the hum of a loaded power line. He was always calculating, always figuring out how to make use of people, always with a commercial end in mind. Everything was for sale. His enthusiasms were strictly mercenary; he seemed incapable of genuine affection. I think he was the loneliest man I've ever met.

He owned a handsome home in Rye, New York, its duplex living room decorated, appropriately enough, with the pelts of dead lions. I remember a publication party he gave to launch one of his books, a celebrity-studded outdoor barbecue on the lawn behind his house with GP in chef's hat and apron presiding over the grill. At the height of the wingding, I left in search of the men's room, and wandered around to the front of the house. An express truck was parked outside, and as I opened the door I saw two movers carrying a trunk from the second floor. Dorothy Binney Putnam, GP's charming and vivacious wife, followed them downstairs, dressed in traveling clothes. "Didn't you know? I'm divorcing George," she said quite casually. "He doesn't need me any more." I strolled back to the party, where GP was gaily spearing frankfurters for a shy young aviatrix named Amelia Earhart. He married her after the divorce was final.

Putnam had a precedent for the book he wanted me to write. In 1921 he had published the highly successful *Cruise of the Kawa,* written by George S. Chappell under his famous nom de plume of Dr. Walter E. Traprock. It was a burlesque epic of South Sea exploration, illustrated with posed photographs of Chappell himself as the intrepid Dr. Traprock, Frank Crowninshield as Herman Swank, a white god, and Heywood Broun as Captain Ezra Triplett, the master of the *Kawa.* My book would be a sort of sequel, GP decided, and with Chappell's generous approval I transferred Captain Triplett to command of the

*Minnie A. Caine,* and gave the Joan Lowell counterpart the name of June Triplett, his daughter. At the suggestion of F.P.A., I titled the book *Salt Water Taffy; or, Twenty Thousand Leagues Away from the Sea.*

By a happy coincidence, Felix von Luckner's old sailing ship was tied up at a Hudson River pier on public exhibit; Putnam leased it for a day, and a group of invited celebrities were piped aboard to be photographed standing at the wheel or climbing around the rigging. GP had persuaded a beautiful debutante from Chicago named Annie Laurie Jacques, later Mrs. Jo Mielziner, to play the part of the heroine, June Triplett. Heywood Broun, despite his unfortunate experience with *Cradle of the Deep,* agreed to pose again as Captain Ezra Triplett. Frank Sullivan, complete with red chin-whiskers and a curved pipe, was loyal old Britches. Reinald Werrenrath, the Metropolitan baritone, was Knut Hansom, the sailor who loved above his station; Clarence Chamberlain was the cabin boy; and among the members of the crew were Percy Crosby, Charles J. V. Murphy, Walter Trumbull, and Donald Ogden Stewart, attired in a fringed admiral's hat and sagging sailor suit as Olaf ("Horrible") Olsen, the ship's bully. Harold Ross was Old Sedlitz, the beachcomber, baring his teeth lecherously at June Triplett (later he signed the picture "H. W. Ross in his biting mood"). Frank Crowninshield, in white robe and sandals and a flowered crown, repeated his role of Herman Swank, the King of the Virgin Isles, surrounded by a bevy of Virgins including Neysa McMein, Elizabeth Cobb Chapman, and Alison Smith, all in the grass skirts and sarongs which constituted the native costume on No-Men Atoll.

One of the most dramatic photographs showed Heywood Broun crouched at the ship's railing, firing a cannon at an approaching waterspout. (The waterspout was skillfully dubbed in by cameraman Harold McCracken.) This thrilling escape

The King of the Virgin Isles (Frank Crowninshield) performs a marriage ceremony for "Horrible" Olsen (Donald Ogden Stewart) and Old Sedlitz (Harold Ross) and their native consorts (Neysa McMein and Elizabeth Cobb Chapman). From *Salt Water Taffy*.

from death was chronicled in Chapter IV of *Salt Water Taffy,*
and gives some idea of the hair-raising suspense of June's
almost incredible autobiography:

> I shall never forget the day that Gladys arrived.
>
> That hot afternoon I had been stationed on the aft'm'st wimpers to
> keep a sharp eye out for the icebergs, which constituted a constant
> menace to shipping around the equator (it wasn't so much the ice,
> actually, as the fact that they were infested with polar bears) when I
> heard the lookout give his familiar cry of warning: "Loooo-ook
> out!" and a moment later, as was his custom, he landed on the back
> of his neck upon the deck. He scrambled to his feet and saluted.
>
> "What is it?" demanded Father.
>
> "I don't know," he replied sheepishly. "I just had a hunch."
> Sailors are very superstitious, and often believe in premonitions of
> disaster. This time his hunch was justified, for no sooner had he
> climbed back to the crow's-nest than I heard his cry again: "Loooo-
> ook out!" and this time he landed on the top of his head.
>
> "Starboard beam port bow aft!" he cried, staggering to his feet.
>
> I saw Father take one look, and his face blanched.
>
> "Strum the m'n'tch!" His voice shook the air. "Avast with the
> poop, and trim the tr'b'lts!"
>
> "Aye, aye, sir!" everybody replied at once.
>
> "Tr'f'g in the blizzzz'm'brghtwch!" bellowed Father.
>
> "Why, surely, sir," replied the embarrassed sailors, running in all
> directions, some hoisting the sails, others reefing them, others
> lowering the anchor or nervously shifting the cargo, while two or
> three sailors in their confusion manned a lifeboat and rowed rapidly
> away to the east.
>
> "Luff up a bit!" roared Father, so I put my arms around a nearby
> sailor and luffed up a bit. Obedience is the first law of the sea.
>
> The wind meantime had commenced to hum with a vicious
> steadiness from starboard, and the sky was rapidly darkened with
> racing clouds. The sea itself had become an ominous black. Over the
> roar of the wind and the excited whispers of the puzzled sailors,
> Father shouted: "Waterspouts to l'rrrrr'w'd!"

I looked where he pointed. As I watched, the clouds and the sea seemed for a moment to meet; and then for the first time I made out a group of objects like huge hour-glasses wandering toward us across the horizon, swaying and writhing and uttering a weird wailing sound that grew louder as they approached. At a glance there seemed to be forty of these strange creatures, their heads lost in the pitching sky, gradually drawing nearer. Father's face went white. Our boat was drifting slowly but surely into their course, and we seemed powerless to avoid disaster.

"Sheet in your jibs!" roared Father. The mate started to reply something, but evidently changed his mind.

"What's happened?" I yelled to him.

"This damned wind is taking us right toward them," he answered. "They'll get our scent any minute."

Now I have heard scientists explain that a waterspout is nothing but a wet cyclone, and that if it were put in an arid section of land, such as Kansas, it would turn into a revolving gust of wind, and probably be elected to the United States Senate. And a fat lot of good that did us right now, with Kansas three thousand miles away and our boat drifting into the very maw of the leading monster. There is nothing more irritating than a scientific paragraph in the midst of a very exciting bit of description, and Father knew it. His lips were pressed together in grim determination, and he never took his eyes once from the approaching waterspout.

"We haven't got a chance!" I heard him mutter.

The leading waterspout was almost upon us, and I could see its hungry maw dripping with anticipation.

Suddenly Father shouted: "June! My rifle!" I found his faithful .22, with which he was wont so often to shoot the sun, and handed it to him with trembling fingers. It was our last chance. The crew and I all held our ears and shut our eyes as he raised it to his shoulder.

Crack! With uncanny aim Father sent a single bullet through the middle of the enemy!

For a moment the waterspout halted dead in its tracks, swaying backward; then slowly it tilted forward and collapsed with a horrible

While June steadies the ship's cannon, courageous Captain Ezra Triplett (Heywood Broun) fires at an approaching waterspout. From *Salt Water Taffy*.

roar. Hundreds of tons of water, fish, seaweed, and a couple of tourists from a nearby steamer descended on our decks, as the stricken waterspout thrashed once or twice feebly, muttered something about taking a letter to "Eloise," twitched convulsively, and disappeared into the sea.

The rest of the herd of waterspouts had halted, evidently nonplussed by this sudden accident to their leader. Now they turned, panic-stricken at the white man's magic, and scattered pell-mell toward the horizon with their tails between their legs. They were gone in an instant, the wind fell, the sun came out, and the two tourists, who were both from Montclair, New Jersey, walked over and introduced themselves to Father.

While the rest of the crew was sweeping up the dead fish, however, I continued to stare at the sea before us. A small wriggling motion had caught my eye. It seemed to rise and fall, moving away from us with uncertain steps in the general direction taken by the vanished herd, and now and again bleating piteously.

"Stop the ship," I called to Father. "I think that's a baby waterspout."

Without a thought of danger I jumped overboard and struck out after my prize. While the crew gathered along the taffrail to watch my chase, I plunged on after the baby spout. I would no sooner swim within easy reach of it, however, than it would flop just out of my grasp. With several swift strokes I overtook it again, but this time it dodged and floundered to the right, whimpering piteously and wriggling in its effort to escape. I overtook it once more. Cornered, it turned upon me and hummed in frantic terror.

I was nonplussed as to the proper way to tame this wild creature, but a sudden idea struck me. I had noticed that the baby spout bore a slight resemblance to a cut-glass vase, similar to the cut-glass vases found in taxicabs. I slyly plucked a nearby sea nasturtium and, reaching up in the air, I thrust this flower down the roof of the little waterspout. My ruse broke its spirit. Slowly I saw its face twist into a grudging smile, and then, as the full flavor of this absurd idea struck home, it broke into a laugh at the ridiculous picture it presented. In this helpless condition I led it back to the ship with ease and hoisted it aboard in a bucket.

After a brief consideration Father allowed me to keep Gladys (as I named her) for my own pet, on condition that I promised not to take her to bed with me. (My bunk was just over Father's.) I kept her in the bucket, feeding her daily on a hundred gallons of sea water; and in the course of time she became thoroughly tame and would spin contentedly for hours.

When Gladys had become thoroughly housebroken — if indeed you can speak of a boat as a "house" — she was allowed the run of the ship, and in the course of time she became a popular favorite with the crew. During hot days in the tropics she would obligingly hang upside down by her heels from the ceiling of the fo'c'sle, while the grateful crew enjoyed a cool shower beneath her. Gladys was as full of fun as "the Old Nick," and her favorite prank of hiding in a sailor's coffee cup and suddenly springing to her full height just as he raised it to his lips never failed to bring a laugh.

Gladys had only one fault. She loved to drink.

One night in Adelaide we two had stopped in at Charlie's for a couple of quick ones, and as usual Gladys had been the sensation of the bar. Gladys' method of drinking was, to say the least, unique. Owing to the peculiar construction of a waterspout, she could not toss down a drink like the rest did, but instead had to sit on the rim of the glass and suck up the drink as if she were a straw. This feat never failed to delight the onlookers, and they would buy as many drinks for her as she would swallow, if you could call it swallow.

Inasmuch as Gladys and I were together, the crowd at the bar would set out another drink for me whenever they ordered a new one for Gladys; and soon I felt my own head spinning. The more I drank, the faster I seemed to spin. My first indication that anything was the matter was when I noticed Gladys had practically stopped whirling.

"Why are you standing still?" I asked her in surprise.

"I'm not standing still," said Gladys. "I'm whirling as fast as ever. You're just going past me so fast that it seems as if I were standing still."

I took another drink.

"You *are* standing still," I told Gladys. "In fact, you're going backwards."

"Maybe you better get her home," one of the sailors whispered to Gladys.

I have no idea how we managed to get back to the ship. My first impression was of following Gladys giddily up the gangplank and coming face to face at the top with something very large and very unpleasant, which was breathing fire and smoke and a series of picturesque oaths. A second glance showed that it was Father.

"Look, I'm a waterspout." I smiled nervously, revolving once or twice to show him what I meant.

For a moment he stared at me, spinning uneasily before him; then in grim silence he seized a length of thick rope and advanced toward me with a terrible frown. I felt that I was in for some rough weather astern. It was Gladys' presence of mind that saved us both. So furious was Father that he did not see her step quickly in front of me; and in his blind rage he seized Gladys by mistake. As he turned her over his knee, his expression suddenly froze, and slowly changed to one of bewilderment. He shifted slightly, then abruptly rose with an embarrassed giggle, dumping the loyal waterspout unceremoniously upon the deck, and hobbled down below to his cabin.

By the time he emerged again in a dry pair of trousers, I was safely hidden in the jizzm'nfch grig, where no one could find me.

The final chapter of *Salt Water Taffy* recorded June's tearful departure from the ship, and the start of her climactic swim from Australia to New York, followed by her father in a rowboat stocked with reams of paper and sharpened pencils. Captain Triplett took the pages of June's autobiography as fast as she wrote them — she averaged fifty words to the minute, despite the handicap of the ship's anchor which she was carrying home as evidence — and handed her fresh sheets of waterproof paper. Her swimming time was set back slightly when she discovered that Richard Halliburton had obtained exclusive

Loyal Old Britches (Frank Sullivan) and June Triplett.
From *Salt Water Taffy*.

rights to swim the Panama Canal, and she had to detour by way of Cape Horn; but she finished the final chapter off the Virginia coast, and Captain Triplett rowed north to deliver it to the printers. He met her again in his rowboat as she entered New York Harbor, beside himself with excitement, and described the maganificent reception which was being prepared for her:

New York is planning one of her famous welcomes, Father says. Banks are being closed, schools suspended, and business houses are shutting down to allow their employees to view the huge parade up Broadway, as I pass through a lane of ticker tape and torn-up telephone books, like a veritable May snowstorm, to be welcomed on the City Hall steps and presented with the keys of the city by the Mayor. After a round of luncheons, speeches, presentations and the like, the day will terminate in a tremendous dinner aboard the *Ile de France* for five hundred editors and critics who will gather together to welcome me back after my record-breaking swim.

Putnam, the supreme showman, had worked out a publicity arrangement with the French Line, and all of New York's leading columnists and critics were invited to a banquet aboard the *Ile de France* on May 29, 1929, the eve of publication day. In the midst of the festivities, there was a commotion on deck, and everyone rushed out to see June Triplett, her oilskins dripping water, climb over the rail triumphantly with a copy of *Salt Water Taffy* in her hand. Home at last!

I never met Joan Lowell, but that was due in part to my expert footwork. I had heard that she was six feet tall and built like a female wrestler, and her one desire in life was to punch me in the nose. Friends took delight in coming up to me in a theater lobby and whispering, "Joan Lowell is here looking for you," and then watching me streak for the nearest exit. Miss Lowell had good reason to be vexed. *The Cradle of the Deep* had been at the top of the non-fiction best-seller list, but a couple of weeks after the publication of my exposé it plummeted out of sight.

Thanks to GP's shrewd promotion, sales of *Salt Water Taffy* mounted steadily, and by midsummer, at the age of twenty-seven, I found myself the author of the nation's number one best seller. Its success, by coincidence, helped to soothe Joan Lowell's ruffled feelings. People who bought my parody wanted to read the original, and bit by bit *The Cradle of the Deep* climbed back into the weekly list — but this time under the heading of fiction.

One sad word in conclusion. That October of 1929 I invested all my royalties in the stock market, just in time for the Wall Street crash. As Heywood Broun said philosophically, when his own savings from forty years in the newspaper business were wiped out overnight, "Easy come, easy go."

# 12

## *Still a Time for Laughter*

DECEMBER 5, 1933, was as festive an occasion as New Year's Eve. Utah had become the thirty-sixth and final state needed to ratify the Twenty-first Amendment, the Prohibition law was revoked, and New York's speakeasies swung their doors open for the first time since 1920. No more basement bells, no more sliding panels, no more thirteen-year-old air. Drinks on the house, boys. Ring out the old era, ring in the new.

That night Jim Moriarty gave a mammoth cocktail party to celebrate repeal. He had moved recently from "109" to the Marlborough House at 15 East 61st Street, next door to Mrs. Payson's town residence. The fashionable address, the marble foyer and broad winding stairs, the crystal chandeliers and rich carpeting were no more elegant than Jim himself, tall and suave and impeccably dressed, mingling affably with his guests and dispensing champagne and caviar with the prodigality of a real-life Gatsby.

All the old Moriarty crowd was on hand. Frank Sullivan and Russel Crouse and Alison Smith. Heywood Broun and Harold Ross. Alva Johnston, a cigarette twitching and occasionally leaping from his long nervous fingers. F.P.A., downing his Martini in a single gulp as if it were medicine. Prince Mike Romanoff, still just a jump ahead of the law. (The immigration officers had tracked him to Marlborough House once, but friends lowered him to safety in the dumbwaiter.) Deems Taylor. Marc Connelly. Edna Ferber and George and Beatrice Kaufman. Don Stewart and Mr. Benchley at a table with Mrs. Parker, demure as a kitten, her claws sheathed.

A gala gathering; but somehow the merriment seemed a little forced, the clink of glasses had a hollow ring. Perhaps we sensed, that night of repeal, that more than Prohibition had died, that a whole way of life was gone forever. Within a few months Marlborough House, like most of the taverns of the Twenties, would be shuttered and silent, deserted by former patrons who would flock instead to gaudy new nightclubs and hotel cocktail lounges. The Golden Age of Humor, uninhibited and irreverent, had drawn to a close; the party was over. Later that evening John Held, Jr., strolled over to join our table. He had set the pattern for the Jazz Age, and it seemed fitting that he should be here to see it end. . . .

Overnight the saxophones stilled, the Black Bottom halted in mid-swing, the laughter was stifled. The climate of the Thirties was more serious, more responsible. The stock market crash, the depression years, the bank closings had jolted the country out of its complacency. Hitler was already casting his long chill shadow across the decade, and there was an increasing sense of tension, of foreboding.

As the national mood sobered, the demand for humor declined. The comic magazines had ridden out the Wall Street typhoon, but now they foundered one by one: *College Humor,* then *Vanity Fair,* scuttled by Condé Nast, then *Life,* taken over for salvage by the Luce empire, then *Judge,* then, after a brief meteoric career, Norman Anthony's *Ballyhoo*. Only *The New York* remained, but its high standard of excellence discouraged young writers, and the lengthy articles and stories and departments left little space for experimenting with unknowns, as Ross had done in the days when White and Thurber and Gibbs were testing their wings. The comedy market was drying up. Back in the Twenties, Don Marquis and F.P.A. had run contributions by unknowns, and their columns had served as a breeding ground for burgeoning talent; but they were gone, and no similar outlets had taken their place. Slowly but surely the production of humor dwindled, and so did the producers. Ross observed sadly, shortly before his death in 1951, "Not one genuine new humorist has emerged in this country since the middle Thirties."

Frank Sullivan, writing in the *New York Times Book Review*, wondered whether the dearth of new fun-makers might be due to what he called "the Moola factor, by which promising young humorists, along with other kinds of promising young writers, are lured into writing for radio, television, or Hollywood by the promise of vast sums of moola, bigger messes of pottage, more imposing gastric ulcers and anxiety neuroses designed to astound psychoanalysts at a distance of thirty couches. . . . No wonder young writers trembling on the verge of becoming humorists think twice and then take a job at $500 a week writing gags for Uncle Milty or Bob Hope. You cannot blame them for trying to collect the maximum dividends on their talents. In the world we live in, they owe it to themselves to earn enough to provide their wives and kiddies with the best bomb shelters money can buy."

There is another reason, Sullivan suggested. Humorists are edgy about seeming frivolous in these troubled times. Their fun-making might be considered trivial and in bad taste, a sort of fiddling while Rome burns; and they try to avoid public reproach by packing a message of Social Significance into their comedy — a worthy ambition, but disastrous to humor. Their feeling of inferiority is understandable, for we tend to regard our comedians with contempt. "The world . . . decorates its serious artists with laurel," as E. B. White wrote, "and its wags with Brussels Sprouts." And Bennett Cerf adds, "We've never given any of our serious prizes to a humorist — the Pulitzer Prize, the National Book Award, the great international Nobel Prize. Somehow the honors never go to the people who make other people laugh."

Whatever the reason, I miss the comedy of the Twenties, and the great comedians whom I knew and loved. F.P.A.'s gruff and pithy comments. Mr. Benchley's generous laugh. The solemn clowning of Ring Lardner, the sweet sad humor of Don Marquis, W. C. Fields's snarling asides (I wonder if any modern producer would have the courage to film that defiant and larcenous old rogue), the pantomime of Buster Keaton. Most of all I miss the incisive satire and parody that used to level its lance against contemporary targets, pricking pretensions, deflating stuffed shirts. I've tried my own hand at parody over the years, but I think it is done best by younger writers. Where are they? When will a new generation of comedians grab the torch from the gnarled hands of yesterday's funnymen as they toddle off to what Frank Sullivan calls the Petroleum V. Nasby Home for Aged and Infirm Humorists?

For we need humor today, as we have never needed it before. I mean the warm and clean and graceful fun of the Golden Decade, the sense of nonsense which would give this careening world of ours some sanity and balance. Now, if ever, is a time for laughter.

# Acknowledgments and Bibliography

THE Golden Age of Comedy was a long long time ago, and most of the great humorists of the Twenties have answered the summons of the Man in the Bright Nightgown; but I am deeply indebted to the remaining handful of stalwarts for their anecdotes and recollections and generous assistance to me in compiling this nostalgic record. My particular thanks to Frank Sullivan, the sage of Saratoga, New York, for lending me his scrapbooks and other pertinent material, and for checking my manuscript; to Dave and Maude Chasen of Beverly Hills, California, for helpful memoirs of the Joe Cook and early Hollywood days; to Marc Connelly, who remembered Dave Clark's lyric after forty years; to Jack Shuttleworth, former editor of *Judge;* to J. Bryan III, connoisseur of humor and good friend; and to Ogden Nash, Nathaniel Benchley, and Katharine and E. B. White for corrections and valuable suggestions.

My gratitude also to the staff of Dartmouth College's Baker Library, who furnished me with the full collections of *Life* and *The New Yorker;* J. Blair Watson, Jr., director of Instructional Services at Dartmouth, who gave me access to his film library; Dorothy Olding of Harold Ober Associates, for her invaluable

advice and encouragement; Michael Clapp of Tyler, Texas, who
labored long and faithfully to collect background material;
Bernard Dougall of Westport, Connecticut, for supplying
anecdotes of the Twenties; Norma Bouchard of Hanover, New
Hampshire, who patiently typed and retyped my manuscript;
and, last but not least, Llewellyn Howland III of Little, Brown
and Company, who first suggested the idea for this volume, and
guided me through its painful period of gestation.

The following books and magazine articles have been most
helpful in my research:

### BOOKS

Anthony, Edward. *O Rare Don Marquis.* New York, Doubleday, 1962.
Anthony, Norman. *How to Grow Old Disgracefully.* New York, Duell, 1946.
Allen, Frederick Lewis. *Only Yesterday.* New York, Harper, 1931.
Allen, Frederick Lewis. *Since Yesterday.* New York, Harper, 1940.
Benchley, Nathaniel. *Robert Benchley.* New York, McGraw-Hill, 1955.
Benchley, Robert. *Chips Off the Old Benchley.* New York, Harper, 1940.
Congdon, Don. *The Thirties.* New York, Simon and Schuster, 1962.
Fitzgerald, F. Scott. *This Side of Paradise.* New York, Scribner, 1931.
Fowler, Gene. *Minutes of the Last Meeting.* New York, Viking, 1954.
Harriman, Margaret Case. *The Vicious Circle.* New York, Rinehart, 1951.
Hart, Moss. *Act One.* New York, Random House, 1960.
Kramer, Dale. *Ross and The New Yorker.* New York, Doubleday, 1951.
Oppenheimer, George. *The View from the Sixties.* New York, McKay, 1966.
Stewart, Donald Ogden. *A Parody Outline of History.* New York, Doran, 1921.
Sullivan, Mark. *Our Times: The Twenties.* New York, Scribner, 1935.
Taylor, Robert Lewis. *W. C. Fields, His Follies and Fortunes.* New York, Doubleday, 1949.
Thurber, James. *The Years with Ross.* Boston, Little, Brown, 1959.
Woollcott, Alexander. *While Rome Burns.* New York, Viking, 1936.

### ANTHOLOGIES

Amory, Cleveland, and Frederic Bradley, eds. *Vanity Fair.* New York, Viking, 1960.
Blum, Daniel, ed. *A Pictorial History of the Silent Screen,* New York, Grosset, 1953.
Blum, Daniel, ed. *A Pictorial History of the Talkies.* New York, Grosset, 1958.
Cerf, Bennett, ed. *An Encyclopedia of Modern American Humor.* New York, Hanover House, 1954.

Griffith, Richard, and Arthur Mayer, eds. *The Movies,* New York, Bonanza Books, 1957.

Meredith, Scott, ed. *The Fireside Treasury of Modern Humor,* New York, Simon and Schuster, 1963.

Munsey, J. B., ed. *The Cream of the Jesters.* New York, Boni, 1931.

Taylor, Deems, ed. *A Pictorial History of the Movies.* New York, Simon and Schuster, 1943.

Untermeyer, Louis, ed. *A Treasury of Laughter.* New York, Simon and Schuster, 1946.

*Vanity Fair Book, The.* New York, John Day, 1931.

White, E. B., and Katherine S. White, eds. *A Subtreasury of American Humor.* New York, Coward-McCann, 1941.

## MAGAZINES AND MAGAZINE ARTICLES

*Life,* 1922–1929.
*The New Yorker,* 1925–1933.
*Vanity Fair,* 1920–1933.

Bryan, J., III, "Funny Man," *Saturday Evening Post,* Sept. 23 and Oct. 7, 1939.

Connelly, Marc. "The Most Unforgettable Character I've Met: Robert Benchley," *Reader's Digest,* May 1965.

Sayre, Joel. "How to Eat Like a Movie Star," *Saturday Evening Post,* Apr. 6, 1957.

Shuttleworth, Jack. "John Held, Jr., and His World," *American Heritage,* Aug. 1965.

Sullivan, Frank. "Well, There's No Harm in Laughing," *New York Times Book Review,* Dec. 16, 1951.

Wheeler, John. "Unforgettable Ring Lardner," *Reader's Digest,* Oct. 1966.

# Index